Tell Me a Story

Tell Me a Story

Using Narratives to Break Down Barriers in Composition Courses

Anthony Tate Fulton
Christopher B. Field
Michael MacBride

ROWMAN & LITTLEFIELD
Lanham • Boulder • New York • London

Published by Rowman & Littlefield
A wholly owned subsidiary of The Rowman & Littlefield Publishing Group, Inc.
4501 Forbes Boulevard, Suite 200, Lanham, Maryland 20706
www.rowman.com

Unit A, Whitacre Mews, 26-34 Stannary Street, London SE11 4AB

Copyright © 2018 by Anthony Tate Fulton, Christopher B. Field, and Michael MacBride

All rights reserved. No part of this book may be reproduced in any form or by any electronic or mechanical means, including information storage and retrieval systems, without written permission from the publisher, except by a reviewer who may quote passages in a review.

British Library Cataloguing in Publication Information Available

Library of Congress Cataloging-in-Publication Data

Names: Fulton, Anthony Tate, 1978– author. | Field, Christopher B., 1980– author. | MacBride, Michael, author.
Title: Tell me a story : using narratives to break down barriers in composition courses / Anthony Tate Fulton, Christopher B. Field, Michael MacBride.
Other titles: Using narratives to break down barriers in composition courses
Description: Lanham, MD : Rowman & Littlefield, 2018. | Includes bibliographical references and index.
Identifiers: LCCN 2017031454 (print) | LCCN 2017041808 (ebook) | ISBN 9781475828801 (electronic) | ISBN 9781475828788 (hardback : alk. paper) | ISBN 9781475828795 (pbk. : alk. paper)
Subjects: LCSH: Narration (Rhetoric) | English language—Rhetoric—Study and teaching. | Storytelling in education. | Education—Biographical methods. | Creative writing (Higher education) | Teacher-student relationships.
Classification: LCC PE1425.F85 (ebook) | LCC PE1425.F85 T45 2018 (print) | DDC 808/.0420711—dc23
LC record available at https://lccn.loc.gov/2017031454

∞ ™ The paper used in this publication meets the minimum requirements of American National Standard for Information Sciences Permanence of Paper for Printed Library Materials, ANSI/NISO Z39.48-1992.

Printed in the United States of America

Contents

Acknowledgments — vii

Introduction: The Role of Stories and Narratives in Composition — ix

Part I: Breaking Barriers — 1

1 Breaking the Ice: The Teacher as "Story" — 3
2 Using Narratives in First-Year Composition Courses to Allow Students to Confront the Traumatic — 15
3 Narratives as Gateways to Reflection — 31
4 Narratives as a Catalyst for Research — 47
5 As the Semester Ends: The Writing Portfolio as Narrative — 57
6 Stories in an Online Environment — 67

Part II: Implications and Conclusions — 77

7 "Why Did You Give *Me* Such a Bad Grade?": Providing Constructive Assessment of Narratives — 79
8 "Yes, But . . .": Establishing a Language Base for Working with Stories — 87
9 Implications for New Teacher Training — 99

Bibliography — 109

Index — 117

About the Authors — 119

Acknowledgments

Anthony thanks his wife, Anne, and two boys for their support, encouragement, and patience, particularly when he kept reminding them, "I have a book to write in a month!" He thanks Sarah Jubar, their editor, for seeing the potential in this project and suggesting that it could be turned into a book. He also thanks his coauthors, Michael and Chris, for their unique ideas, humor, and expertise. Thanks also to Professor Sarah Doherty Gottschall for insightful conversations about teaching with stories.

Michael thanks his wife and two boys for both giving him space and happy distractions during the writing process. He also thanks his coauthors, Chris and Anthony. Who knew a little conference presentation would lead to this?

Chris thanks his wife, Kelli, and his son, Jonathan, for their steadfast support. He also thanks his coauthors, Anthony and Michael, for being patient with his tendency to wait until the very last minute to finish his homework. He would also like to thank Dr. Kimberly King-Jupiter and the staff of the 2017 Tennessee State University Summer Writing Retreat for their assistance and funding during the composition of some sections of this work. Finally, he would like to thank his dear friend and colleague, Dr. Heidi Williams, for putting up with his ramblings and for encouraging and inspiring him to be a better teacher.

Introduction

The Role of Stories and Narratives in Composition

The three authors of this book met on a day filled with stories, both uplifting and terrifying. On an uncharacteristically cool August morning, Michael, Chris, and Anthony gathered, along with nearly 25 of their peers, in a classroom in Faner Hall, an imposing concrete structure on the campus of Southern Illinois University–Carbondale. That morning in 2007 marked the start of an intensive, two-week training workshop for new graduate teaching assistants (TAs), set to teach composition that fall.

Gathered in the tightly spaced rows of desks were master's and doctoral students in both literature and rhetoric and composition, as well as several Master of Fine Arts (MFA) students. The experience level of this diverse group ranged from no teaching experience to three to five years of teaching composition and literature.

Anthony and Chris, who met years before as TAs at another university, worked as a full-time lecturer and adjunct, respectively, for two years before enrolling in the graduate program at SIUC. Sitting near the back of the room, they quickly befriended Michael, who had several years' experience teaching composition and literature. All three were nervous and excited to begin this new venture.

The assistant administrator of the writing program, clad in bright red pants and black-and-white saddle shoes, led the morning's introductory sessions. Energetic and positive, he led the group through several short warm-up writings and discussions, putting everyone at ease. He was an adept discussion leader, balancing all of the comments and ensuring that everyone had a chance to speak and ask questions.

Finally, the assistant director, along with several experienced TAs who were serving as small-group leaders for the training, convened a session on dealing with disciplinary problems. He began with a story.

In this situation, a young TA, similar to those listening to the story, had a student who refused to put away her cell phone. The student continued to text and even answer calls during class, despite the instructor's insistence that she adhere to the cell phone policy outlined in the syllabus. Not wanting to let the student take control of the class, the instructor attempted to confiscate the student's cell phone, wrestling it from her hands. When the student threatened violence, using vulgarity, the instructor left the classroom and called campus police on his own cell phone. Campus police removed the student from the classroom, and the class session continued.

The assistant director intended to use the story as a case scenario to open a debate on handling discipline issues. However, before he could ask the group to evaluate the instructor's actions in the story and brainstorm other ways to handle the problem, someone else told a similar story. This triggered a succession of stories that happened to TAs in the past, each one more extreme than the previous one. Tales of in-class fistfights and students being physically pulled out of a classroom by campus police were shared. Stories of suspension and expulsion abounded.

Several of the MFA students, who were generally more inexperienced teachers than some of their peers in MA and PhD programs in composition and literature, began to express concerns. Chris and Anthony exchanged glances. At their previous institution, the most severe issues they faced were the occasional plagiarism issue and call from an angry parent. Was the situation far worse at a public institution? They began to wonder.

Registering the panic in the room, the assistant director brought the exchange to a halt and noted that many of the stories shared were very extreme cases, and that most of the undergraduate students in composition are hardworking, and follow established policies. He then expertly guided the discussion back on track, but there was a palpable tension and murmuring in the room for the remainder of the session.

That tension faded as the week wore on, and the TAs broke into small groups to review the first unit of the standardized composition syllabus: the literacy narrative. Discussing how to teach this assignment brought the experienced and inexperienced teachers together. The MFA students offered creative and fun lesson ideas, while others shared strategies for grading and responding to student work.

These two instances from one training workshop show the power of stories in the classroom. Stories have the power to expose problems, as well as ignite creativity and thinking. They can infuse energy into a classroom during a long session, and also bring together students of various ages, races, genders, and levels of experience. On the other hand, as the first story illustrates, stories can create fear and tension, raising awareness to problems.

In addition to emphasizing the power of stories, these two instances underscore the connection between stories and barriers. The nightmare-scenario stories, while creating tension, highlighted potential barriers and exposed concerns and fears as the TAs were heading into the semester. As the work began, the literacy narrative assignment broke down potential barriers of age and experience. It leveled the field and emphasized the expertise of individual groups.

This book attempts to harness that power to help students grow and develop as writers. It argues that stories and narratives can be utilized in the composition classroom, specifically first-year composition (FYC), to break down barriers. Throughout a given semester, stories and narratives can help students in composition courses to overcome academic, personal, and creative barriers, establishing a space to develop as writers and thinkers. Providing theoretical approaches, practical methods, and implications for using stories in FYC, this book explores the versatility of stories as teaching tools.

TEACHING AND STORYTELLING

In his memoir on 30 years of teaching in New York City public schools, McCourt (2005) recounted his decision as a young teacher to tell students about his life growing up in Ireland. Initially, he reminded himself that he should be teaching and not wasting time telling stories. Ultimately, though, he concluded that "storytelling is teaching" (p. 26). Before detailing how stories can break down barriers, it is essential to situate this book within explorations of stories as teaching tools throughout various historical contexts and in academia. This section will provide historical context, reviewing relevant primary and secondary texts.

Historically, storytelling, as rooted in the oral tradition, has been entwined with teaching for centuries. Within Native American and African American storytelling traditions, storytelling becomes a form of imparting lessons, as well as a way to inspire and entertain.

Ollerenshaw and Lowerey (2006) highlighted the Seneca Nation as a key example of storytelling as a learning tool. Storytellers used stories to model behavior, pass on tribal knowledge and history, and shape collective memories. During "the unthinkable hardships of slavery," Grace, Smith, and Hinchman (2004) explained that slaves created "personal narratives, animal tales, narratives about the supernatural, the tall tale, and the freedom tales" to inspire and to endure (p. 483).

The benefit of stories as teaching tools is their ability to present issues in creative and memorable ways. Slave narratives illustrated the power and potential of stories to educate by painting the intangible (or unthinkable) into vivid experiences. Narratives, like "Narrative of the Life of Frederick Douglass" (1987), educated readers—including skeptics—about the horrors of slavery. Douglass disclosed names and locations, as W. Lloyd Garrison acknowledged in the preface to the narrative, allowing readers to confirm the truths behind the story. Grace, Smith, and Hinchman (2004) noted that these narratives also emphasized the perseverance of dignity "in the face of inhumanity" (p. 483).

Analyzing other primary sources through history reveals a key instructional method of narratives: teaching through example. War memoirs from the twentieth century, like slave narratives, utilized this method effectively. These straightforward memoirs that lack any direct editorializing on the horrors of war (Sassoon, 1930; Webster, 2002) can educate through images and precise, sensory details.[1] On this point, O'Brien (1990) suggested in his collection of short stories on Vietnam that a true war story "does not instruct" but will embarrass, shock, and remain difficult (pp. 68–69).

While some texts illustrate the benefits and methods of stories as teaching tools, other innovative texts can expand our conceptions of narratives and how they are constructed. Journals and diaries, as well as photo collections, scrapbooks, and letters have the potential to create reflective chronicles of events and ideas (Stevens & Cooper, 2009). Texts such as *The Letters of John and Abigail Adams* (2004), Anne Frank's *Diary of a Young Girl* (1967), and—in the digital age—Jenny Lawson's 2017 blog, *The Bloggess* (http://thebloggess.com/), can teach readers about the unique ways that larger narratives can be woven throughout shorter, collected texts.

In academia, educators have drawn on various kinds of narrative texts to engage students, share experiences, and deepen cultural knowledge. Teaching through storytelling, or "narrative pedagogy," is utilized not just in literature and composition studies, but also in a myriad of disciplines, including nursing, education, and business (Davidson, 2004, p. 184).

Storytelling in nursing education can help students visualize specific clinical situations (Davidson, 2004), value diversity (Branch, Min, & Anderson, 1999; Koening & Zorn, 2002), and prompt reflective thinking (Ramsey, 2000). Preservice teachers in education can employ storytelling techniques to develop reflective strategies and connect theory to practice (Binks, Smith, Smith, & Joshi, 2009), as well as increase self-efficacy with technology (Heo, 2009). In business, storytelling can "illustrate management principles such as decision-making, leadership, group dynamics, power and politics" (Harbin & Humphrey, 2010, p. 99).

In the field of rhetoric and composition, specifically, stories weave through scholarship and practice. Scholars and historians have relied on storytelling within the last several decades to foster unity and cohesion in the field. Scholarly histories, documenting stories of the field's origins (Brereton, 1995; Connors, 1997; North, 1987), presented the complexities of past events to potentially provide greater clarity about the present and future. According to Connors, building a fire and swapping stories around that fire, figuratively speaking, crystalize the field's storytelling tradition, helping to create a professional identity and common history (p. 18).

Stories of specific times and places, such as Henze, Selzer, and Sharer's (2007) examination of Penn State's writing program in the late 1970s, fill in the gaps of larger rhetorical histories (p. 4). Classroom-based ethnographies have also experimented with narratives, chronicling the experiences of individual students and a group of students enrolled in composition (Hunt, 2002) and in courses across the curriculum (McCarthy, 1994). Providing context and rich detail, these smaller stories can also present implications for the field at large. In all, these histories show the value of narratives as teaching tools in the field.

In the composition classroom, as in courses across the disciplines, narratives contribute to students' development as writers and readers. Writing narratives, Hillocks (2007) observed, "allows students to contribute to the body of literature they will study, understand more fully how the works of professional writers are constructed, and learn techniques that will be useful in other kinds of writing" (p. 1). In reading narratives, Goldblatt (2017) observed that students often "refer to narratives with which they can readily connect as 'relatable,' and they often prize that quality above logical persuasion or even emotional appeals of other kinds" (p. 439).

Perhaps the most direct and debated application of stories in composition is the literacy narrative. Scholarship on literacy narratives has increased significantly in the 2000s, due in part to the genre's multidisciplinary nature.[2] To study literacy narratives is to examine literacy, reflection, empowerment, culture, human behavior, and many other issues.

Literacy narratives on a basic level, Soliday (1994) explained, recount situations involving language acquisition. More specifically, "literacy narratives become sites of self-translation where writers can articulate the meanings and the consequences of their passages between language worlds" (p. 511). Although there is no prescribed formula, literacy narrative assignments in composition, Alexander (2015) observed, often require a narrative of events and an analysis of the significance of those events. Unlike war memoirs and other narratives that define through example, literacy narratives often build in a direct analytical component.

Scholars have noted the many benefits of assigning literacy narratives. Reflection plays an integral role in constructing these worlds of language and making sense of those worlds (Alexander, 2015; Bar-On, 2007). Thus, literacy narratives and narrative-based assignments have the potential to promote self-reflection and facilitate reflective skills (Alexander, 2015; Bar-On, 2007; Brady, Corbie-Smith, & Branch, 2002; Levett-Jones, 2007). However, as

Alexander argued, while scholarship agrees on the potential of literacy narratives to foster reflection, there is much debate as to how best to foster deep reflection.

In addition to promoting reflective skills, scholars have found that literacy narratives have the potential to give voice to cultural diversity (Soliday, 1994). As forums for "cultural expression," in which students engage with multiple viewpoints, literacy narratives, in turn, can build student confidence (Corkery, 2005, p. 50). Literacy narratives, through a synthesis of narrative and reflection, can analyze and even challenge educational practices and structures (Bishop, 2000; Daniell, 1999; Ryden, 2005).

Despite these potential benefits, scholars have noted some limitations of the genre. First, instructors occasionally must address perceptions that narratives and stories are "easy." Taking this point further, critics of the genre, Goldblatt mused, find memoirs and narratives "embarrassing and unworthy of academic attention" (p. 439). By intersecting culture, literacy, analysis, and reflection, as the research discussed above has suggested, narrative essay assignments can be sufficiently rigorous.

Another noted limitation of literacy narratives is the "literacy myth," the common belief that obtaining the ability to read and write directly correlates to economic, professional, personal, and academic success and improvement (Eldred & Mortensen, 1992; Graff, 1979). Perpetuating the myth of literacy as a cure-all, Bryson (2012) observed, can obscure other crucial factors related to social, personal, and economic problems.

Moreover, since the genre is new for many students and, as Ryden (2005) argued, is not often found outside of school, some writers may defer to existing narrative structures, like the literacy myth, as opposed to exploring their own contexts of language acquisition.

For the authors of this book, one concern is the perception that narratives and stories are confined only to a designated literacy narrative essay. Many popular and useful composition texts include specific chapters devoted to writing narratives (Cooley's *Back to the Lake*, 2012) and literacy narratives (Bullock's *The Norton Field Guide to Writing*, 2013), as well as employ narrative essays throughout to illustrate other genres and concepts.

However, genre terms used to identify assignments in composition—which many of these books echo, like "compare and contrast" and "argument essay"—could send a message to students, unintentionally, that these essays and the processes used to construct them are separate from narratives.

USING STORIES TO BREAK DOWN BARRIERS

Literacy narratives, however, are only a piece of the overall landscape. This book project developed from a presentation at the National Council of Teachers of English (NCTE) conference in 2014. The conference theme that year was "Story as the Landscape of Knowing." Program Chair K. G. Short (2014) observed that stories are "the glue," binding the community together "in our shared journeys of professional inquiry" (p. 3). These inquiries, thanks to the versatility of stories, take shape in many ways.

Several of the presentations aimed at the college level discussed approaches to the literacy narrative, specifically using the genre for students of diverse backgrounds. However, a majority of the presentations looked at other ways stories can inform teaching practices in regard to technology, encouraging diversity, rhetoric, interdisciplinary approaches, and visual literacy. From using stories to sharpen analysis and reflection to helping students develop focused stories in college application essays, the landscape was varied.

Literacy narratives and single-narrative essays can be extremely useful. However, this book aims to extend the conversations of the conference and the versatile research noted above by forwarding other innovative ways that narratives and narrative elements can have a role in shaping first-year students' reading and writing experiences.

This book argues that narratives and stories hold great power, and that power can be integrated in a more comprehensive way into FYC to break down key barriers that students may encounter. It balances theory and practice to offer tangible approaches, lessons, and methods for using stories and narratives to break down obstacles in FYC. Additionally, it offers practical implications for using stories and narratives as teaching tools.

IDENTIFYING BARRIERS THROUGH NARRATIVE-BASED INSTRUCTION

Students in FYC face many barriers. On the first day of class, the authors of this book often tell stories primarily to break the ice and introduce themselves. These stories also attempt to put students at ease by acknowledging, both tacitly and explicitly, some of the key barriers that they may face in composition. These short stories highlight the many issues that this book will examine.

In his classes, Anthony often introduces himself by describing his first job out of college. He worked for a children's book publisher that featured child authors. Anthony had the thankless job of writing rejection letters to the children whose manuscripts were not chosen for publication. Because the publisher wanted to make the experience educational, he had to draft an individualized letter offering specific feedback, using literary terms. Despite the stress, this job offered early training in responding to other writers about their work. This story often elicits chuckles, but also sparks a discussion about the frustrations and rewards of writing.

Specifically, this story facilitates a discussion on assessing writing and providing individualized feedback. Students often encounter instructor feedback that is, as Sommers (1982) observed, rubber-stamped and interchangeable; this "uniform code" emphasizes rules over offering individualized suggestions for revision (p. 237). Scholarship has found that students prefer comments that are framed in specific ways and consider the context of the situation (Dohrer, 1991; Straub, 1997). Producing specific commentary—either instructor feedback or peer reviews, as Anthony's anecdote illustrates—can be stressful and confounding.

Discussions about offering feedback and applying specific concepts typically emphasize barriers related to language. As Hagemann (2003) posited, students' grades often reflect their knowledge of content and use of academic English, based on Standard Academic English (SAE). The language of academic discourse, specifically editing symbols and abbreviations (Straub, 1997), terms that are open to multiple interpretations (Mullin, Reid, Enders, & Baldridge, 1998; Nelms & Dively, 2007), and the often-dense language of writing assignments (Simon, 1991) can create barriers to clarity and understanding.

The recent writing about writing movement (Downs & Wardle, 2007) can complicate issues further. While this approach moves composition research from behind the scenes to the center of the classroom, it does introduce another strain of new terms and theoretical concepts for students to negotiate. Thus, terms like "felt-sense," "metacognition," and "social constructionism" become introduced alongside composition terms such as "signal phrase," "persuasion," and "block quotation."

Like Anthony, Chris draws on his professional experience to put students at ease. When Chris worked in marketing, he witnessed a fellow worker get fired over a comma splice. Of course, the real story is more complicated, as the comma splice was the final mistake in a long line of critical mistakes. Chris uses the story to reassure students that while many of them think they are going to fail a composition class because of minor errors, they will not, in fact, fail because of comma splices. In his class, they work on those aspects of writing in order to get them prepared for high-pressure situations, like the one from the story.

Grammar anxiety, as this short tale illustrates, is certainly a barrier for many students. However, students come to composition courses with many concerns. Students' attitudes and previous experiences with concepts, methods, and activities can often color their willingness to engage (Charney, Newman, & Palmquist, 1995). To use a popular slang term, they have "baggage."

For example, Robinson and Burton (2012) observed this issue in using self-reflection to assess writing-intensive courses. Respondents in their study distrusted peer reviews, which suggested that "students may carry baggage of past negative peer review experiences into their advanced writing courses" (p. 516). This "baggage," then, could disrupt students' processes and potentially lead to resistance of certain activities.

Chris's short tale also highlights the misperception that teaching writing equates to teaching grammar. As Clark (2003) explained, politicians, parents, and students often demand more emphasis on grammar when discussing writing skills in schools. The problem of misperception extends beyond grammar instruction. In addition, compositionists often must negotiate views that expository writing cannot be creative (Karnezis, 1998) and that all academic writing is a form of "bullshit" (Eubanks & Schaeffer, 2008). Stories, along with other methods, as this anecdote illustrates, have the potential to counter misconceptions and ease anxieties.

Finally, Michael's introductory story hints at the ways that narratives can break down potential barriers. To get his students to think critically right out of the gate, Michael often tells true stories that, at first glance, read like tall tales. The time that Eddie Vedder, the lead singer for the rock group Pearl Jam, bought Michael orange juice, is a prime example. Years ago, Michael went to a Pearl Jam show, where his friend was a guitar tech for the opening act. Vedder came out and bought them drinks. Because Michael was as "sick as a dog" at the time, Vedder bought him orange juice instead of alcohol.

Interdisciplinary scholarship on the first day of class revealed that teachers can lose credibility and set an improper tone by just taking roll, reading through the syllabus, and introducing the assigned texts (Dorn, 1987). Many scholars (Dorn, 1987; Gaffney & Whitaker, 2015; McGinley & Jones, 2014) concurred that first-day activities—from questionnaires to icebreakers—can increase instructor credibility and student engagement. Michael's opening story works against those first-day barriers, as it is similar to Gaffney and Whitaker's (2015) notion of using rumors about an instructor to inject humor and honesty on the first day of class.

In addition to serving as an icebreaker, this anecdote is also used to introduce critical thinking and reading skills. For instance, Michael's students often think that the story is fake because it goes against certain expectations and preconceived notions about rock stars. Thus, it invites reflection on and analysis of these notions and triggers a dialogue about false assumptions. As Hillocks (2007) noted, stories contribute to reading skills by fostering reflection, and serving as a basis for discussion, critical responses, and questioning.

This brief review presents just some of the key barriers that this book will address. Obviously, students will encounter a number of other hurdles, based on their experiences, needs, and concerns. While this book cannot address all these issues, it focuses on the key issues addressed above to illustrate the possibilities and pitfalls of stories as teaching tools for teachers of writing.

HOW TO USE THIS BOOK

Instructors teaching FYC and other writing-intensive courses at colleges, universities, and community colleges are the primary target audience for this book. High school English teachers who wish to use narratives and stories as a way to transition into college-level writing may also find it to be a practical resource.

Both experienced and new teachers could benefit from this book; however, it would be especially beneficial to new graduate teaching assistants with creative writing backgrounds who are teaching composition for the first time. Based on their collective experiences in training new TAs, the authors found that many new teachers, specifically those in MFA programs, felt comfortable teaching literacy narrative essays and other narrative-based essays in composition. Thus, this book could help new teachers utilize stories and narratives to teach new and unfamiliar subject matter.

Finally, this book could also serve as a resource for teachers working in departments that have deemphasized narrative-based and description-based essays. Anecdotally, some English departments, including those of two of the authors, have discouraged narratives in favor of more argument-based essays. As noted, while this book argues for the benefits of literacy narratives and other narrative-based essays, it primarily emphasizes alternative ways to use stories and narratives as powerful learning tools in writing classes. Thus, this book aims to be a practical resource for instructors working under specific requirements and in specific contexts.

The title, *Tell Me a Story: Using Narratives to Break Down Barriers in Composition Courses*, essentially informs this book's structure. Building on this foundation, each chapter will focus on different kinds of barriers that students might encounter in FYC and other composition courses, and offers tangible, practical ways to use narratives to resolve, and potentially remove, those barriers.

Another feature of this book is the inclusion of multiple stories and narratives, drawn from the authors' personal and professional experiences to illustrate specific ideas and concepts. A book about stories, we posit, should include stories. By including these stories, we hope to provide concrete illustrations of specific constructs and claims.

Collectively, the chapters will move through a loose sequence of a typical composition course, from the first day of class to completing research for a culminating research project. The idea behind this approach is not to present a prescriptive, canned composition sequence, but to illustrate the various ways that narratives can be used as instructional tools at various points in a given semester to solve a diverse array of problems. The book will conclude with implications and recommendations for assessing narratives and building a language base for working with narratives.

These chapters will, ultimately, tie together to show how narratives can be used at various points in a typical semester, but the chapters can also be used independently. For instance, the chapter on how literacy narratives can help students negotiate past trauma focuses on recent work with trauma theory and then applies those concepts in sample assignments and lessons; theory and application are contained within a single, accessible chapter.

Thus, this book aims to be flexible and versatile. Stories and narratives are powerful tools that can jump-start an argument and support an argument. The chapters will explore this idea to offer practical lessons, methods, and strategies for incorporating stories and narratives into every aspect of the writing process.

CHAPTER GUIDE

The first part of this book focuses on specific barriers that students face in the composition classroom. Chapters 1 and 2 examine methods for confronting and tearing down common obstacles. The first chapter focuses on creating a strong classroom environment through icebreakers and short exercises that frame the teacher as a story. Chapter 2 offers a specific view of literacy narratives and their power to help students confront the traumatic.

The next three chapters focus on ways that stories and narratives can unlock specific skills. Using an interdisciplinary approach, chapter 3 explores how stories and narratives can create pathways to meaningful student reflections on writing. Chapter 4 presents a sample narrative and assignment to illustrate how stories can serve as engaging starting points for research. Chapter 5 focuses on the writing portfolio—specifically, the reflective introduction or the cover letter for the portfolio—as a "narrative" demonstrating the story of the changes the writer has made in her or his writing process.

Chapter 6 expands the focus to the online composition classroom, detailing the role of narratives in shaping a tight-knit online community. Drawing on principles from recent research, it offers sample assignments to foster collaboration at various points in an online course.

The second part of this book provides implications for employing stories and narratives throughout a composition course. Chapter 7 contends that rubric construction is an essential element in reassuring writers in FYC courses that when they are sharing sometimes deeply personal information in narratives, the teacher is assessing the ability of the narrative to meet the demands of the genre, rather than judging the writer personally.

Chapter 8 qualifies some of the claims posed in part 1 by arguing that teachers must create a language base for talking about and using stories in the classroom. Finally, chapter 9 provides implications for new teacher training. Specifically, it offers strategies for employing story-based discussions in courses and training programs for new and experienced composition instructors.

NOTES

1. In his introduction to Webster's 2002 memoir, S. E. Ambrose commented that the book can educate readers about war and combat, as it "brings back a place and a time, a sense of commitment, the feeling of 'we are all in this together' as the United States and her allies fought for freedom" (p. x).

2. Looking at just the ProQuest thesis and dissertation database gives some potential insights into the growth of scholarship on literacy narratives. Searching through the 3,772,474 theses and dissertations in English (as of 2017) for "literacy narratives" yields 636 results from 1984 to 2017. Those break down this way: 1980–1989: 1; 1990–1999: 48; 2000–2009: 242; 2010–2019: 345. Of course, while "literacy narrative" is a specific term used to describe a type of writing and writing assignment, it is possible that some of these works are drawing on a different conception of the term that deviates from the common usage.

REFERENCES

Adams, J., & Adams, A. S. (2004). *The letters of John and Abigail Adams*. F. Shuffelton (Ed.). New York, NY: Penguin.

Alexander, K. P. (2015). From story to analysis: Reflection and uptake in the literacy narrative assignment. *Composition Studies*, *43*(2), 43–71.

Ambrose, S. E. (2002). Introduction. In D. K. Webster (Ed.), *Parachute infantry: An American paratrooper's memoir of D-Day and the fall of the Third Reich* (pp. ix–xvi). New York, NY: Delta.

Bar-On, T. (2007). A meeting with clay: Individual narratives, self-reflection, and action. *Psychology of Aesthetics, Creativity, and the Arts*, *1*(4), 225–236.

Binks, E., Smith, D. L., Smith, L. J., & Joshi, R. M. (2009). Tell me your story: Reflection strategy for preservice teachers. *Teacher Education Quarterly*, *36*(4), 141–156.

Bishop, W. (2000). *The subject is reading*. Portsmouth, NH: Boynton/Cook.

Brady, D. W., Corbie-Smith, G., & Branch, W. T., Jr. (2002). "What's important to you?": The use of narratives to promote self-reflection and to understand the experiences of medical residents. *Annals of Internal Medicine*, *137*(3), 220–223.

Branch, M., Min, D., & Anderson, M. (1999). Storytelling as a teaching-learning tool with RN students. *ABNF Journal*, *10*(6), 131–135.

Brereton, J. C. (Ed.). (1995). *The origins of composition studies in the American college, 1875–1925: A documentary history*. Pittsburgh, PA: University of Pittsburgh Press.

Bryson, K. (2012). The literacy myth in the digital archive of literacy narratives. *Computers and Composition*, *29*, 254–268. http://dx.doi.org/10.1016/j.compcom.2012.06.001

Bullock, R. (2013). *The Norton field guide to writing* (3rd ed.). New York, NY: Norton.

Charney, D., Newman, J. H., & Palmquist, M. (1995). "I'm just no good at writing": Epistemological style and attitudes toward writing. *Written Communication*, *12*(3), 298–329.

Clark, I. L. (2003). *Concepts in composition: Theory and practice in the teaching of writing*. Mahwah, NJ: Lawrence Erlbaum.

Connors, R. J. (1997). *Composition-rhetoric: Backgrounds, theory, and pedagogy*. Pittsburgh, PA: University of Pittsburgh Press.

Cooley, T. (2012). *Back to the lake*. (2nd ed.). New York, NY: Norton.

Corkery, C. (2005). Literacy narratives and confidence building in the writing classroom. *Journal of Basic Writing, 24*(1), 48–67.

Daniell, B. (1999). Narrative of literacy: Connecting composition to culture. *College Composition and Communication, 50*(3), 393–410.

Davidson, M. R. (2004). A phenomenological evaluation: Using storytelling as a primary teaching method. *Nurse Education in Practice, 4*(3), 184–189. http://dx.doi.org.ezproxy.pgcc.edu/10.1016/S1471-5953(03)00043-X

Dohrer, G. (1991). Do teachers' comments on students' papers help? *College Teaching, 39*(2), 48–54.

Dorn, D. S. (1987). The first day of class: Problems and strategies. *Teaching Sociology, 15*(1), 61–72.

Douglass, F. (1987). Narrative of the life of Frederick Douglass. In Gates, H. L. (Ed.), *The Classic Slave Narratives* (pp. 243–331). New York, NY: Mentor.

Downs, D., & Wardle, E. (2007). Teaching about writing, righting misconceptions: (Re)envisioning "first-year composition" as "introduction to writing studies." *College Composition and Communication, 58*(4), 552–585.

Eldred, J. C., & Mortensen, P. (1992). Reading literacy narratives. *College English, 54*(5), 512–539.

Eubanks, P., & Schaeffer, J. D. (2008). A kind of word for bullshit: The problem with academic writing. *College Composition and Communication, 59*(3), 372–388.

Frank, A. (1967). *Diary of a young girl*. New York, NY: Doubleday.

Gaffney, J. D. H., & Whitaker, J. T. (2015). Making the most of your first day of class. *The Physics Teacher, 53*, 137–139. http://dx.doi.org/10.1119/1.4908079

Goldblatt, E. (2017). Don't call it expressivism: Legacies of a "tacit tradition." *College Composition and Communication, 68*(3), 438–465.

Grace, C. M., Smith, K., & Hinchman, K. (2004). Exploring the African American oral tradition: Instructional implications for literacy learning. *Language Arts, 81*(6), 481–490.

Graff, H. J. (1979). *The literacy myth: Cultural integration and social structure in the nineteenth century*. New Brunswick, NJ: Transaction.

Hagemann, J. A. (2003). Helping students acquire the language of the academy. In C. R. Boiarsky (Ed.), *Academic literacy in the English classroom*, (pp. 131–144). Portsmouth, NH: Boynton/Cook.

Harbin, J., & Humphrey, P. (2010). Teaching management by telling stories. *Academy of Educational Leadership Journal, 14*(1), 99–106.

Henze, B., Selzer, J., & Sharer, W. (2007). *1977: A cultural moment in composition*. West Lafayette, IN: Parlor Press.

Heo, M. (2009). Digital storytelling: An empirical study of the impact of digital storytelling on pre-service teachers' self-efficacy and dispositions towards educational technology. *Journal of Educational Multimedia and Hypermedia, 18*(4), 405–428.

Hillocks, G., Jr. (2007). *Narrative writing: Learning a new model for teaching*. Portsmouth, NH: Heinemann.

Hunt, D. (2002). *Misunderstanding the assignment: Teenage students, college writing, and the pains of growth*. Portsmouth, NH: Boynton Cook.

Karnezis, G. T. (1998). Reclaiming "creativity" for composition. In D. Starkey (Ed.), *Teaching writing creatively* (pp. 29–42). Portsmouth, NH: Boynton/Cook.

Koening, J. M., & Zorn, C. (2002). Using storytelling as an approach to teaching and learning with diverse students. *Journal of Nursing Education, 41*(9), 393–399.

Levett-Jones, T. L. (2007). Facilitating reflective practice and self-assessment of competence through the use of narratives. *Nurse Education in Practice, 7*, 112–119.

McCarthy, L. P. (1994). A stranger in strange lands: A college student writing across the curriculum. In C. Bazerman & D. Russell (Eds.), *Landmark essays on writing across the curriculum*, (pp. 125–154). Mahwah, NJ: Erlbaum, 1994.

McCourt, F. (2005). *Teacher man*. New York, NY: Scribner.

McGinley, J. J., & Jones, B. D. (2014). A brief instructional intervention to increase students' motivation on the first day of class. *Teaching of Psychology, 41*(2), 158–162.

Mullin, J., Reid, N., Enders, D., & Baldridge, J. (1998). Constructing each other: Collaborating across disciplines and roles. In C. Peterson, M. Haviland, M. Notarangelo, L. Whitley-Putz, & T. Wolf (Eds.), *Weaving knowledge together: Writing centers and collaboration* (pp. 152–171). Emmitsburg, MD: NWCA.

Nelms, G., & Dively, R. L. (2007). Perceived roadblocks to transferring knowledge from first-year composition to writing-intensive major courses: A pilot study. *WPA: Writing Program Administration, 31*(1–2), 214–240.

North, S. (1987). *The making of knowledge in composition: Portrait of an emerging field.* Upper Montclair, NJ: Boynton.

O'Brien, T. (1990). *The things they carried.* New York, NY: Broadway.

Ollerenshaw, J. A., & Lowery, R. (2006). Storytelling: Eight steps that help you engage your students. *Voices from the Middle, 14*(1), 30–37.

Ramsey, C. A. (2000). Storytelling can be a valuable teaching aid. *Association of Operating Room Nurses, 72*(3), 497–499.

Robinson, T. A., & Burton, V. T. (2012). The writer's personal profile: Student self-assessment and goal setting at start of term. In T. M. Zawacki & P. M. Rogers (Eds.), *Writing across the curriculum: A critical sourcebook* (pp. 508–523). Boston: Bedford/St. Martin's.

Ryden, W. (2005). Conflicted literacy: Frederick Douglass' critical model. *Journal of Basic Writing, 24*(1), 4–23.

Sassoon, S. (1930). *Memoirs of an infantry officer.* New York, NY: Coward-McCann.

Short, K. G. (2014). *NCTE 104th annual convention program.* Washington, DC: NCTE.

Simon, L. (1991). De-coding writing assignments. *The History Teacher, 24*(2), 149–155. Retrieved from http://www.jstor.org/stable/49412

Soliday, M. (1994). Translating self and difference through literacy narratives. *College English, 56*(5), 511.

Sommers, N. (1982). Responding to student writing. *College Composition and Communication, 33*(2), 148–156.

Stevens, D. D., and Cooper, J. E. (2009). *Journal keeping: How to use reflective writing for learning, teaching, professional insight, and positive change.* Sterling, VA: Stylus.

Straub, R. (1997). Students' reactions to teacher comments: An exploratory study. *Research in the Teaching of English, 31*(1), 91–118.

Webster, D. K. (2002). *Parachute infantry: An American paratrooper's memoir of D-Day and the fall of the Third Reich.* New York, NY: Delta.

Part I

Breaking Barriers

Chapter One

Breaking the Ice

The Teacher as "Story"

The traditional classroom, with a podium or instructor desk at the front and student desks looking toward the podium, establishes a dynamic of "us" (instructors) and "them" (students). Students are well aware of this dynamic before they even enter the classroom, but when they do enter that space, it is reinforced yet again.

Instructors can do many things to help lessen the division. They can sit on the front desk, facing the group in a more conversational approach. They can rearrange the student desks in a circle and occupy one of those desks themselves. However, unless the instructor arrives early to do these things before the students arrive, by the time the desks are shifted and positions are taken, authority is already established.

Authority is an important part of the classroom, but it is also a double-edged sword. On the one hand, it establishes control and ensures that the instructor is unquestioned when discussions may derail or feedback on an assignment may not be well received. On the other hand, authority also makes it more difficult for students to feel comfortable approaching their instructors and to feel the connection necessary to really engage with the material.

This chapter discusses how icebreakers, self-disclosure, and a little sleight of hand can help to establish a classroom environment where students feel connected to their instructors and the course, and are encouraged to think critically about all the sources presented to them—instructor included.

ICEBREAKERS

It is hard to say how many college classes begin with an icebreaker, because there does not appear to be any formal study investigating that question. It is clear from the research, regardless of the type of class (English, psychology, physics, or sociology; online or face-to-face) that icebreakers are encouraged and, when used effectively, can quickly create class cohesion.[1]

Not only are icebreakers a way of breaking the tension created by the "us and them" dynamic, and a welcome distraction from the "serious" material to come, but study after study shows that icebreakers perform three essential functions.

First, icebreakers allow students to begin forming learning communities by getting to know one another and finding like-minded peers.[2] Second, contrary to the knee-jerk reaction that a "fun" activity might diminish the seriousness of an instructor and diminish his or her authority, these relatively simple activities actually help build an instructor's credibility.[3] Finally, icebreakers build rapport between the student and the instructor, which helps students feel connected to the course.[4]

While there is agreement about the usefulness and effectiveness of icebreakers in the classroom, there is no such consensus about *which* icebreaker works best. This chapter focuses on using the common icebreaker "two truths and a tall tale" (sometimes called "two truths and a lie") as the means to begin a conversation with students that can accomplish the above functions as well as challenge students to think critically of the sources around them.

Two Truths and a Tall Tale

On the surface, two truths and a tall tale appears to be a simplistic activity. Typically, an instructor begins by writing three statements on the board and informing the students that two of the statements are true and one of them is false. Their task is to identify the false statement. This activity requires students to go out on a limb and risk being wrong. If they have never taken a course with the instructor before, then they have very little information to work with. They can examine the classroom, they can look at how the instructor has chosen to dress or present him- or herself to the class, and they can examine any books or a syllabus, if one is presented to them.

After a short time to deliberate, the instructor then reads each statement, asking students to raise their hands for the statement that they believe is the false one. Once the votes have been tallied, a conversation should ensue where students disclose the logic they used to make the choice they did. Students who have participated in this icebreaker before may offer reasons such as: the false statement was written last, since it is harder to write; or, that the instructor may anticipate that the students have guessed the false statement to be the last one, and has chosen to bury the false statement at the beginning or middle of the list.

Particularly astute students may notice sentence structure differences between true statements and false ones, and other students may simply guess. Regardless of the reason the student chose the statement he or she did, thinking through the logic behind the choice is an essential element of this icebreaker. If students can correctly deduce a truth from a lie with this limited information, it follows that, when they have more information, they should similarly be able to reach correct conclusions.

In addition to this non-obvious aspect of the icebreaker, each of these statements—true or not—reveals something about the instructor to the students. Instructors may choose to reveal former jobs, famous people they have encountered, ridiculous situations they have found themselves in, places they have visited, languages they speak, or any number of possible facts. The lies also reveal things about the instructor—for instance, how deceptive or tricky he or she can be, and how imaginative he or she is. Now that the instructor has modeled the activity for the students, it is the students' turn.

Student should be given some time to create their own list of three statements, and encouraged to create statements that reveal some kind of character trait or something unique about them. While statements such as "I have two brothers" (or "I am 18 years old") certainly do reveal information about the student, these are less interesting and conversation generating than a statement like "I have traveled to three continents." It is important that students are reminded that this activity will require sharing what they have written, and so they should be selective about the truths they reveal and be careful about what they write.

Once students have generated their lists, they should form small groups and perform a version of the large-group activity the instructor has modeled. At the end of the allotted time, students should be prepared to introduce one other member of the class and reveal the most interesting piece of information that they have learned about him or her. This way, in addition to getting to know one another, students feel responsible for representing one another fairly in front of the class, and the instructor can compile a list of facts about each student that will help him or her with name retention.

With this activity, which can be used in any classroom, students have learned to think critically about the information around them, formulated an argument for (or at least the logic behind) why their conclusions might be correct (demonstrating reflective awareness in the process), met several new students, and learned a few things about the instructor.

While instructors might value the first two benefits of this activity, students certainly value the last two. For them, they have made connections. They no longer feel so alone in the classroom. This connection is not limited to the peers they have met—it extends to the instructor as well. Even in this limited self-disclosure, the "two truths and a tall tale" activity humanizes the instructor for the student, and in the process, helps to lessen the burden of the "us and them" dynamic.

SELF-DISCLOSURE

It is understandable that an instructor would want to maintain a professional distance from his or her students, but self-disclosure can occur at varying degrees and does not necessarily require becoming friends with the students. Something as simple as the icebreaker described above goes a long way to making the students think of the instructor more dynamically, instead of just an authoritarian grading machine. The scholarship about the relative closeness of relationships between students and instructors has included examples suggesting the "importance of a close, caring teacher-student relationship" (Furrer, Skinner, & Pitzer, 2014, p. 102).

The majority of this research discussed K–12 classrooms, but the scholarship on teacher-student relationships in the college classroom surprisingly noted that college students reported "a sense of connection with teachers helps students feel like they belong at the institution" (Duberstein, 2009, n.p.); "teacher immediacy usually conveys messages of inclusive and caring" (Rester & Edwards, 2007, p. 46); and those "who viewed an instructor's website with high levels of mediated immediacy, including forms of self-disclosure, reported high levels of motivation and effect of learning, indicating positive attitudes toward the class and the teacher" (as cited in Mazer, Murphy, & Simonds, 2007, p. 2).

Additionally, Goldstein and Benassi (1994) showed that "teacher self-disclosure is positively associated with student participation" (p. 215), and later studies on classrooms in the fields of communications[5] and psychology[6] supported their conclusion.

Perhaps most telling, Micari and Pazos (2012) reported that it is in the most difficult courses that students would benefit from a close relationship with their instructor: "[T]here is evidence in the literature to suggest that the way students feel about their relationship to the professor may play an even larger role than many faculty know. . . . In especially difficult courses, students often have fewer personal resources to rely on for support, motivation, and so on—and so the student-faculty relationship takes on a special prominence" (p. 41).

In their study, Micari and Pazos (2012) found that "the more a student felt he or she had a positive relationship to the professor . . . the higher the student's final grade. While this relationship was significant, it was small. . . . A positive relationship to the professor also predicts students' confidence in their ability to do well in the course" (p. 45). It is important to distinguish between a "positive relationship" and a friendship.

At no time has the scholarship advocated befriending students, but rather the use of strategic self-disclosure to present an empathetic, caring, engaged professional. As with any technique, too much of a good thing can prove disastrous. For instance, the research suggested that students typically resent an instructor who uses the classroom for his or her soapbox.[7] But, for instructors who walk that line carefully, the rewards are great for students and for instructors as well.

As Lad Tobin wrote in "Self-Disclosure as a Strategic Teaching Tool: What I Do—and Don't—Tell My Students" (2010), "I reveal to my students enough about my personal history, experiences, and values to feel a sense of integration and integrity . . . I teach most effectively when the self I perform in the classroom is not totally out of sync with the self I generally take myself to be in my non-teaching life" (p. 204). Performing an authentic, or a more authentic, version of yourself allows for a more natural, comfortable classroom environment.

To sum up, self-disclosure allows students to feel connected to the instructor and class and, in turn, also helps the instructor feel connected to the class and students. This shared connectivity results in greater participation from the students, a willingness to approach the instructor during office hours or for questions after class, an increased confidence in students' ability to achieve course goals, and increased motivation to complete the course and feel a part of the university community.

INSTRUCTORS AS SOURCES

Rosamond King, in "They Ask, Should We Tell? Thoughts on Disclosure in the Classroom" (2013), stated that "for many years as a preventative measure, on the first day of class, I would tell the students, 'I am not a text for you to read' . . . I explained it was inappropriate for them to 'read' me and my life in the same way we uncover literary texts" (pp. 101–102). But why not? Instructors are simply one more text for students to make sense of. Students need to be able to determine our biases, anticipate our expectations, and weigh the information they receive from us against the other sources that surround them.

For King, it's not a matter of hiding, or of being "ashamed of [her] personal life," but rather resentment in that she suspected her "colleagues who are white and/or male and/or older . . . rarely, if ever, [are] asked similar questions" (p. 102). King added that "direct disclosure often draws more time and attention to the professor's personal life, not less" (p. 102). This, as stated in the previous section, can be true if it is overused.

The key, then, is to find the correct balance to allow each student to make a personal connection and provide enough information to identify biases and determine credibility with regard to the instruction they are about to receive. This information is vital throughout the course, but never more so than on the first day of class.

As much of the scholarship about the first day of class has suggested, the first day—indeed the first week of class—is an important trying-out period. It is, as Dorn (1987) reminded us, "an encounter among strangers" (p. 61). Students must decide quickly whether this class and instructor are right for them. If they are not, then those students need to drop the class and find one that is a better fit.

In order to better prepare students to make this decision, Michael begins his classes with the "two truths and a tall tale" icebreaker to help the students feel connected to one another and to begin to feel connected to him. Then at the end of class, he assigns his students a "Google your instructor" activity.

This assignment requires students to perform three tasks: find 10 facts about the instructor, cite which source provided that information in the student's preferred documentation format (MLA, APA, Chicago, etc.), and come to class prepared to discuss what they found and how they knew that information referred to their instructor and not someone with the same, or similar, name.

While instructors like King were nervous about inviting students to "read" their personal lives in this way, the simple fact is that many students do inquire, and have already inquired, about their instructors. Sometimes this occurs online, with a simple Google search or a site like ratemyprofessor.com (or similar sites), and sometimes informally, from family or friends, fraternity or sorority brothers or sisters, or information provided by the college or university.

With the cost of education and the time commitment required to complete a course, it would be foolish to make such an investment without a little research (even though many students make such decisions based simply on scheduling demands). By inviting students to dig, Michael simply initiates a conversation in which he has the opportunity to confirm or refute information that students find.

While on the surface this activity seems to students to be an amusing opportunity to snoop and put their instructor on the spot, it provides important information to the instructor, helps to break down the "us and them" dynamic further (increasing the students' connection to the class and instructor), and forces students to engage in critical thinking. Because, especially on the first day of class, students have relatively little information to go on, they must engage all the material they encounter critically, and flex their research muscles.

Some students could interview an instructor's coworkers, or ask friends, family, or fraternity or sorority brothers and sisters, but relatively few do. Instead, they opt to use the Internet and search engines. In doing so, depending on how common the instructor's name is, a student is confronted with an enormous amount of information to sift through. Unlike well-known topics that they might be assigned to research in other classes, there is probably not a wealth of information about their instructor online.

When students return to class with their lists in hand, Michael asks students what they found. Typically, they begin hesitantly, unsure if they found the correct information and not wanting to embarrass themselves, or the instructor, so early in the semester. Steadily they gain confidence, and factoids begin to fly from their mouths as the instructor writes them on the board. It is important not to comment during this time, and just to let students unload their findings.

Once the information begins to ebb, it is then time to evaluate the information. If students are careful, they may have found the instructor's age, former places of employment, maybe social networking pages (Facebook, Twitter, LinkedIn, etc.), a professional webpage, a blog, published articles or books, information from ratemyprofessor.com (or similar sites), perhaps a copy of a CV or resume, and so on. More than the simple information itself, it is important to ask what can be derived from this information.

What does someone's age, for example, reveal? If the instructor is young, they may be reluctant to reveal how close their age is to their students, but many benefits come from this relative closeness of age. Young instructors can draw from examples that are more relevant to students, and students are more likely to approach youthful instructors during their office hours or after class, simply because there is less differentiation.

Being older does immediately lend credibility, whether that is well deserved or not, but it also means that older instructors must work harder to form connections with their students. Regardless of what the number is, age is frequently something that students wonder about, particularly with younger or youthful-looking instructors, and so addressing it in the first week gets that out of the way.

Each piece of information a student finds helps to reveal that the instructor is more than an automaton that spews forth lectures, randomly generates activities, evaluates papers, and spits out grades—but it is also an opportunity for a story. This interaction is akin to an interview, where each student is deciding if this class is a good fit. Students may ask about some of the publications, or conferences where the instructor has presented a paper. These topics reveal the professional interests of the instructor, potentially establish the instructor's credibility, and reveal that this instructor is, like the student, also engaged in academic pursuits and critical thinking.

These are not only opportunities to humanize the instructor, but also a chance to reveal something about the profession. Each piece of information the student finds also tells the instructor something about that student. How hard did he or she dig? How creative was that student with his or her research? Did that student simply choose random information, or was he or she more selective about the items included on his or her list? How careful was that student in making choices about which sources to trust?

When students aren't careful, Michael reports that they have informed him that he was played by Sean Connery in the film *Darby O'Gill and the Little People* (1959); he is a horror fiction writer; he is a subject of a song for which there is a ring tone available online; or that his name is spelled variously: Michael MacBridge, Michael McBride, Michael McBridge, Micheal MacBride, and Micheal McBride. Each of these misfires is also an opportunity for a conversation and a chance to talk about the critical thinking required to investigate a topic you know very little about.

In addition to the various conversations this activity introduces, it also allows instructors the opportunity to evaluate a student's level of comfort with documentation. Requiring students to create a "works cited" page, references page, or bibliography makes students responsible for disclosing where they found the information and allows the instructor the chance to identify how much class time should be set aside to address proper documentation. Sometimes students coming into a class possess a surprising level of comfort and accuracy with regard to documentation, requiring little further instruction.

In addition to potentially tailoring lessons about documentation to fine-tune trends identified in these lists of sources, the lists also present an opportunity to address other possible sources they could have used, and to showcase the variety of sources their peers utilized. When students begin to think more widely about sources, they begin to use a better variety of sources in their work.

Because they now think of their instructor as a source (potentially in a variety of topics), students begin to see the college or university as a place full of walking information. They begin using personal interviews more, and utilize primary sources (such as talking to a campus police officer about crime on campus, or to an instructor who specializes in the topic on which they are writing a paper). Sometimes the students even engage in creating their own surveys or questionnaires to gather their own data, to see how their data compare to national studies or information they find in print or online.

This kind of research, of course, offers its own problems to an instructor as well. How do you verify that the student actually conducted such an interview? How do you verify the information the interviewee provided? Typically, particularly with first-year composition students, students are reluctant to pursue this kind of research without guidance or confirmation from the instructor, and are unlikely to invent information. But if students are interested in engaging in primary research, there are two very important discussions to have.

First is the importance of balancing primary and secondary research—too much primary research can create issues of credibility for a project. Second is the need for proper etiquette when approaching other instructors, workers on campus, or people in general for interviews—make an appointment rather than just show up in someone's office; be polite; create thoughtful questions ahead of time; ask first if you want to record the conversation; take notes; and thank the person for his or her time.

Whether or not students actually conduct interviews, generating interview questions can be a useful activity. Not only does this provide practice about what makes for a good question, but these questions can also serve to direct the research for students.

By engaging their sources more carefully, and being aware of the variety of sources around them, students start to realize why certain sources are more effective for certain kinds of information. If they do conduct a personal interview, then the students see a face behind the information and know that they need to cite that person, instead of just utilizing Wikipedia or some other faceless website. Living sources provide additional clues about credibility through the level of comfort and body language; again, something not present when dealing with print or online material.

CONCLUSION

Rather than starting the class with the typical introduction about the instructor's background, professional interests, and the like, the "Google your instructor" activity places the onus on students to find relevant information and provides students the opportunity to ask the questions they want to know. What starts out as a seemingly random activity to collect information about their instructor turns into something that, hopefully, students will carry with them beyond the walls of this one class: think critically about resources, everything is a source, instructors are merely human, and be proactive in your education.

NOTES

1. Undoubtedly there are other examples for other areas of study, but a quick survey revealed essays in journals specific to the teaching of psychology, physics, sociology, and English.

2. This is perhaps best exemplified in Chlup and Collins (2010): "icebreakers encourage participation by all, helping a sense of connection and shared focus to develop" (p. 34). But this idea is also repeated in nearly all the scholarship: Dorn (1987), Boyle and Rothstein (2003),

Wilson and Wilson (2007), Shadiow (2009), Svinicki and McKeachie (2011), McGinley and Jones (2014), and Gaffney and Whitaker (2015).

3. As in the previous note, this concept is repeated in nearly all the studies. But Gaffney and Whitaker (2015) most thoroughly investigated the idea of what they coined "face work." In short, any activity that "saves face," they postulate, builds credibility. The authors suggest that icebreakers and impromptu question-and-answer sessions require "courage on the part of the instructor because they involve risk" (p. 138). This risk, and the courage to overcome it, demonstrates an instructor's "willingness to stand in that face threatening situation" and "models how to navigate such situations and demonstrates that they are necessary for growth" (p. 138).

4. As stated in the previous notes, this is a common trend in the scholarship. However, all later scholarship seems to build on ideas similar to Dorn (1987), who reminds all instructors that the first day of class in particular is a meeting of strangers, and "as relative strangers to the setting, students will oscillate between remoteness and intimacy, hesitation and uncertainty, distrust and trust" (p. 62). Dorn suggests there are five questions that instructors need to address in order to put students at ease: (1) What are we doing here? (2) How will we accomplish what we are doing here together? (3) What will the instructor be like, and how will the instructor organize the class? (4) Are there any questions? and (5) Who are you? (pp. 65–66). The best and most efficient way to address most of these questions, Dorn suggests, is through icebreakers.

5. See Mazer, Murphy, and Simonds (2007), Rester and Edwards (2007), and Miller, Katt, Brown, and Sivo (2014).

6. See Wilson and Wilson (2007), and McGinley and Jones (2014).

7. Miller et al. (2014) provide a concise review of the scholarship about overuse of self-disclosure in their essay. Additionally, Russ, Simonds, and Hunt (2002) report that students viewed instructors who addressed their sexual orientation in the classroom as "less credible" than straight instructors, or those instructors who did not disclose information about his or her sexual preference (p. 316).

REFERENCES

Boyle, E., & Rothstein, H. (2003). The first class sessions: Engaging students immediately. Chapter 12 in *Essentials of college and university teaching: A practical guide* (pp. 61–67). Stillwater, OK: New Forums Press.

Chlup, D. T., & Collins, T. E. (2010). Breaking the ice: Using ice-breakers and re-energizers with adult learners. *Adult Learning, 21*, 34–39.

Dorn, D. S. (1987). The first day of class: Problems and strategies. *Teaching Sociology, 15*(1), 61–72.

Duberstein, A. (2009). Building student-faculty relationships. *Academic Advising Today, 32*(1). Retrieved from http://www.nacada.ksu.edu/Resources/Academic-Advising-Today/View-Articles/Building-Student-Faculty-Relationships.aspx

Furrer, C. J., Skinner, E. A., & Pitzer, J. R. (2014). The influence of teacher and peer relationships on students' classroom engagement and everyday motivational resilience. *National Society for the Study of Education, 113*(1), 101–123.

Gaffney, J. D. H., & Whitaker, J. T. (2015). Making the most of your first day of class. *The Physics Teacher, 53*(137), 137–139. http://dx.doi.org/10.1119/1.4908079

Goldstein, G. S., & Benassi, V. A. (1994, December). The relation between teacher self-disclosure and student classroom participation. *Teaching of Psychology, 21*(4), 212–217.

King, R. S. (2013). They ask, should we tell? Thoughts on disclosure in the classroom. *The NEA Higher Education Journal, 29*(Fall), 101–111.

Mazer, J. P., Murphy, R. E., & Simonds, C. J. (2007). I'll see you on "Facebook": The effects of computer-mediated teacher self-disclosure on student motivation, affective learning, and classroom climate. *Communication Education, 56*(1), 1–17.

McGinley, J. J., & Jones, B. D. (2014). A brief instructional intervention to increase students' motivation on the first day of class. *Teaching of Psychology, 41*(2), 158–162.

Micari, M., & Pazos, P. (2012). Connecting to the professor: Impact of the student-faculty relationship in a highly challenging course. *College Teaching, 60*(2), 41–47.

Miller, A. N., Katt, J. A., Brown, T., & Sivo, S. A. (2014). The relationship of instructor self-disclosure, nonverbal immediacy, and credibility to student incivility in the college classroom. *Communication Education, 63*(1), 1–16.

Rester, C. H., & Edwards, R. (2007). Effects of sex and setting on students' interpretation of teachers' excessive use of immediacy. *Communication Education, 56*(1), 34–53.

Russ, T. L., Simonds, C. J., & Hunt, S. K. (2002). Coming out in the classroom . . . an occupational hazard?: The influence of sexual orientation on teaching credibility and perceived student learning. *Communication Education, 51*(3), 311–324.

Shadiow, L. K. (2009). The first day of class: How it matters. *The Clearing House, 82*(4), 197–200.

Svinicki, M., & McKeachie, W. J. (2011). Meeting a class for the first time. Chapter 3 in *McKeachie's teaching tips: Strategies, research and theory for college and university teachers* (13th ed.), (pp. 19–25). Belmont, CA: Wadsworth.

Tobin, L. (2010). Self-disclosure as a strategic teaching tool: What I do—and don't—tell my students. *College English, 73*(2), 196–206.

Wilson, J. H., & Wilson, S. B. (2007). The first day of class affects student motivation: An experimental study. *Teaching Psychology, 34*(4), 226–230.

Chapter Two

Using Narratives in First-Year Composition Courses to Allow Students to Confront the Traumatic

When M. H.[1] first approached Chris about writing about her sexual assault for the literacy narrative assignment in his Composition I course, he didn't quite know how to react. While he generally modifies the literacy narrative assignment to broadly define "literacy," which allows students to write about a time when they learned a process, as opposed to a literacy narrative strictly focused on the acquisition of skills related to reading and/or writing, he was initially worried about how well this topic would fulfill the goals of this assignment.

He envisioned the nightmare scenario of the student pouring out some of the most painful and traumatic moments of her life to try to convey those feelings to her reader, only to find that her English teacher had marked up the entire paper for being off topic. Chris knew from experience working with trauma studies in his research that such a scenario could result in the student being even more traumatized because of his insensitivity.

There were also the added worries that could lead to the student re-experiencing the trauma while she was writing about it, a situation that he knew he did not possess the requisite training to handle. Finally, there were the classroom mechanics to consider. He generally requires several peer reviews and peer workshops leading up to the submission of a draft, and he didn't want to put the student in a position where she felt obligated to share such a deeply personal story with classmates who might not respond appropriately.

However, along with all his concerns, Chris knew that there was no choice but to explore the possibility of allowing her to write about her experience, because of the healing potential it presented. Chris's first step in considering the request was to make sure that M. H. was not currently in any danger. This step was a natural reaction, as M. H. had approached him with her request during office hours, and he wanted to make sure that she was okay before they even continued.[2]

Many universities have made their teachers mandatory reporters in the wake of the Jerry Sandusky sexual assault scandal at Penn State University, so it is generally good practice for teachers to check their school's policies if they are at all unsure about what their obligations are in such a case. In this case, though, M. H. assured Chris that she was safe, the authorities had been notified, and her attacker had been punished and was no longer a threat to her.

Chris then asked M. H. how she considered this experience material for a literacy narrative. He read over the assignment prompt with her, combing through it line by line just as he had done with her class the day before. Once they had finished reviewing the prompt, M. H. explained the purpose of the assignment to Chris and how she thought her experience satisfied the prompt.

Her response was that she planned on writing about how she learned about the practice of "slut shaming" following her assault. She explained that in the wake of her attacker's arrest, many people at her high school took her attacker's side and started harassing her via social media. Her response, aside from deleting her social media accounts, was to try to learn more about this practice—the verbiage, the motivations, other contexts where it is employed, how to deal with it, and so on—as a method for coping with and understanding her own assault.

Chris was floored. Her explanation showed him that she envisioned the writing process for this essay as yet another mechanism for trying to understand and deal with her assault. Thus, they quickly dealt with the other issues that initially concerned him. For the peer reviews, she would work with a friend of hers who was in the same class and whom she trusted, and she assured Chris that she was currently in counseling, so he wouldn't be called on any time soon to serve as a de facto therapist—and he was left to ponder how this situation had come about.

Before M. H. approached him with this idea, he knew that some of his students had experienced traumatic situations—they are, after all, human; however, because he had never been confronted with a situation like this, he had never stopped to consider just how much their lives might have been shaped and molded by trauma. Instances like this illustrate how narrative writing in first-year composition courses can allow students to testify to traumatic impact as a method of potentially working through the traumatic event.

As noted in this book's introduction, literacy narratives and other narrative-based assignments provide outlets for reflection and analysis, as well as offer a space in which writers can challenge themselves and their educational histories. Scholars (Corkery, 2005; Soliday, 1994) have documented the ways that literacy narratives can allow students to develop academic identities and even situate themselves within academic structures and discourses. Specifically, the literacy narrative genre, Corkery suggested, prompts students to "interpret or translate their experience to suit their position as a student" (p. 51).

This chapter extends that conversation by arguing that literacy narratives can help students confront painful and traumatic experiences that may inhibit personal, academic, and professional growth. Thus, it will offer specific applications of literacy narratives and other narrative-based assignments.

THEORETICAL CONTEXT FOR WRITING ABOUT TRAUMA IN COMPOSITION COURSES

In adopting narratives to allow students to explore trauma, the work of Peter N. Goggin and Maureen Daly Goggin in their essay, "Presence in Absence: Discourses and Teaching (in, on, and about) Trauma" (2006) is particularly useful. This essay—which is one chapter in Shane Borrowman's collection, *Trauma and the Teaching of Writing* (2006)—builds on noted trauma theorist Dominick LaCapra's (2001, 2004, 2009) designations of writing trauma and writing about trauma.

Goggin and Goggin defined writing trauma as "a working through, and acting out, by those who are first-degree witnesses . . . that is, those who experienced the traumatic event firsthand" (p. 34). They recalled the words of Dori Laub (1995), who claimed, "The testimony is inherently a process of facing loss—of going through the pain of the act of witnessing, and of the ending of the act of witnessing—which entails yet another repetition of experience of separation and loss" (as cited in Goggin & Goggin, 2006, p. 35). Bearing witness, then, can become therapeutic by expressing the loss, but also reinforces the absence felt by the loss.

Writing about trauma, on the other hand, "consists of discourses that draw on, comment on, and interpret first-degree testimony" (Goggin & Goggin, 2006, p. 35). These individuals, such as psychologists who treat patients who have suffered through a traumatic event, deal with exposure to firsthand narratives of trauma.

Goggin and Goggin (2006) added two additional categories: metadiscourse on writing (about) trauma, and writing during trauma. For metadiscourse on writing (about) trauma, Goggin and Goggin explained that it "refers primarily to scholarly discourses that explore questions concerning the complex relationships between trauma and writing" (p. 36). Their own writing, then, would fall under this category, as would this chapter and any other scholarly attempt at exploring trauma.

Finally, for writing during trauma, Goggin and Goggin (2006) classified it as "all those discourses generated during a time of trauma that are not necessarily directly related to the trauma but cannot help but be affected, and in some way to respond to, and be shaped by, the trauma" (p. 36). This category, which is arguably the most intriguing part of Goggin and Goggin's theory, claims that due to its insidious nature, trauma will still influence writing, even if its impact is not immediately recognized.

This chapter, which is focused on providing students the opportunity to write literacy narratives and other kinds of narratives to deal with traumatic events, will, of course, focus primarily on the writing trauma category; however, before we turn our attention to specific ways that we can use writing trauma in the classroom, it is first necessary to acknowledge the inherent difficulties in doing so.

The most obvious difficulty, and one that Goggin and Goggin explored at length, is that the students are writing in a composition classroom rather than under the supervision of a health care professional. The solution to this problem is that students must not be forced to write narratives about traumatic experiences. The key here is to make narrative assignments accessible to write about traumatic experience if students wish, but not to mandate that students write about trauma before they are ready to do so.

If students come to the decision to write about traumatic exposure on their own, the teacher must encourage them to do so only if they are in treatment or have been treated by a health care professional, and the teacher must check in with them frequently throughout the writing process to monitor their well-being.

EXAMPLES OF FYC WRITING ASSIGNMENTS THAT ALLOW STUDENTS TO EXPLORE TRAUMA

In FYC courses, there are multiple approaches to exploring trauma. There does not need to be an explicit connection to trauma in the theme of the course; however, if students wish to write about issues connected to trauma, instructors can allow them to do so if the conditions described above are satisfied.

For example, the theme of Chris's course in which M. H. wrote her literacy narrative was "American popular culture." This meant that students were free to address this theme from any angle, and they were not pressured or prompted to explore it from a strictly trauma-centered perspective. As the sample assignments discussed below illustrate, there are multiple levels of support for students who choose this approach.

For the literacy narrative assignment (see textbox 2.1), Chris has constructed the prompt in such a way as to allow students to either write a traditional literacy narrative where practices related to reading or writing are foregrounded, or they may approach the assignment with broader parameters where students are free to interpret literacy as knowledge acquisition—specifically, how they learned a set of skills related to a process. In preparation for writing this literacy narrative, Chris also incorporates several informal writing assignments to allow students to practice using elements of narratives.

TEXTBOX 2.1. UNIT 1: LITERACY NARRATIVE

Context: When we hear the term "literacy," we are used to thinking about it in terms of reading and writing. However, in a literacy narrative, this term can be broadened to examine how we acquire new knowledge of and skills related to a certain area. The other major component of a literacy narrative is indicated in the name of the assignment: the narrative, which involves telling a story. Thus, in short, a literacy narrative is a story about how you learned a specific lesson.

With the generalized theme of this class—American popular culture—in mind, for your literacy narrative you should focus on telling the story of a time in your life where you learned new skills related to an area of American popular culture. Furthermore, you should also discuss how the acquisition of these skills allowed you to access a new community. While this essay involves you telling a story about yourself, which would seem easy at first glance, this assignment can be deceptively difficult because it asks you to reflect on something you would not normally think about: your practices relating to knowledge acquisition.

Assignment: Write a three- to four-page literacy narrative for an audience of your peers, in which you tell a story about a time when you attempted to learn something related to American popular culture, and how learning these skills either allowed you greater access to a community or prevented you from accessing a new community because of an inability to learn these skills.

Remember that for this assignment, you should a) tell a story instead of writing an informative or research-based essay, b) use vivid details in order to allow your reader to visualize the scene, and c) emphasize the significance of this event, which includes conveying a clear understanding of the learning process that you experienced.

> **Audience:** Your peers. This means that you should write in a style that is appropriate for this audience.
>
> **Format:** This essay should be double-spaced, in Times New Roman font, and at least three pages in length.

For example, one of the informal assignments Chris typically uses is a homework assignment where students are asked to go to a location of their choosing and to write a narrative of what they observe happening around them during a 15-minute time period. This exercise has two aims. First, students get to practice constructing a narrative in chronological order. The students typically utilize rough "And then . . ." transitions to mark the passage of time in these narratives, so this gives Chris the opportunity to also work on integrating alternative transitions to break up the repetitive structure.

The other goal for this assignment is that it allows students to practice integrating vivid details in their narratives. As part of the in-class discussion of these narratives, Chris will ask students to read their informal narratives to the class. If he hears a student use a vague description, for instance, when a student says that a person was wearing a "nice" shirt, then he will encourage the student to incorporate a more vivid description based on sensory experiences. Thus, the description of the "nice" shirt, upon careful prodding, may become a description of a "slightly wrinkled, light-blue T-shirt."

This kind of scaffolding using informal assignments is particularly necessary in dealing with traumatic narratives because details from the traumatic memory may have been lost due to repression.[3] The informal assignments, then, can be invaluable for providing a model for students to use when they are attempting to recall memories from the traumatic event.

To refer back to the example of the observation exercise, Chris stresses to his students that they can use this exercise as a model for recalling events—traumatic or not—that they plan to focus on for their literacy narratives. He also reminds them that it may be necessary to attempt to recall—to observe in retrospect—the events multiple times to be able to recall all the vivid details and plot points they will need to accurately construct their literacy narratives.

In this Composition I class, Chris has also found that an extra-credit assignment (see textbox 2.2) that he offers is a natural and organic influence for inspiring traumatic narratives. For this extra-credit assignment, Chris offers his students the opportunity to produce a creative work that takes one of four forms:

1. Students may produce a short story that describes one instance from the past year in their lives;
2. Students may produce a compilation of four poems that they have written about an event or multiple events from the past year in their lives;
3. Students may write, illustrate, and color a comic book focusing on one event from the past year in their lives;
4. Students may compile a mix compact disc of a minimum of 10 songs that somehow relate to one event or multiple events in the past year of their lives.

TEXTBOX 2.2. EXTRA-CREDIT OPTIONS

You have the option of doing an extra-credit assignment in which you discuss the past year of your life. You may choose *one* of the following options when designing your project:

- Compile a CD with 10 songs that describe the past year. If you choose this option, you must also provide a track listing containing each artist's name, the title of the song, and a short description (minimum two or three sentences) for each song, explaining its importance. Length: 10 songs and a description for each song.
- Write a comic book describing at least one major event in your life that shaped the past year. If you choose this option, you must provide relatively intricate artwork (not just stick figures). You must also provide a one-page, double-spaced explanation of the event and why you thought this medium was a good option for expressing this story. Length: At least six pages for the comic book and the one-page description.
- Write a short story or a poem in which you focus on one event from the past year. If you choose this option, you must also provide a one-page, double-spaced explanation of the event and why you thought this medium was a good option for covering this event. Length: At least three pages for the story or four poems (each poem must cover a different event), and a one-page description.

You will notice that each option includes a writing component. *You must have all of the components to receive credit for the assignment.* The writing component should be formatted according to the format for essay assignments outlined in the course policy sheet.

It must be noted that for each of these creative extra-credit options, students must also provide written narratives explaining the significance of each event and why the author chose this medium (as opposed to the other options for this creative assignment). For example, if a student chooses to compile the mix CD—by far the most popular option—then she or he is responsible for providing a hard copy of the CD, a track listing to identify all the song titles and the artists included on this CD, and an explanation of how each song relates to the event(s) the student is focusing on, with an additional explanation of why the student chose this creative extra-credit option.

Chris originally started offering this extra-credit assignment before he realized how accessible it was for writing about trauma. It was only after several semesters of offering this assignment that Chris started noticing a trend. While the students were given completely free rein to come up with the focal points that they used for their creative assignments, Chris noticed that many people used these assignments to recall events where they were either harmed or endangered.

For instance, a common theme that started to emerge was the inability to deal with a now fractured romantic relationship. While there were variations on this theme—perspectives ranged from bitter feelings due to the romantic partner's unfaithfulness to coming to terms with the end of a first same-sex relationship—these narratives suggested that the students thought of this creative writing assignment as a potentially therapeutic option for safely working through unresolved emotions tied to the event(s).

Once again, Chris did not, and has never, volunteered trauma as a subject for the students to adopt when they were approaching this extra-credit assignment. The responses that focused on attempts to resolve traumatic memories, then, have evolved completely organically, with no obvious or intended encouragement from the instructor.

Chris acknowledges, though, that in hindsight he can see how the students may have independently arrived at the same decision to focus on traumatizing events in their extra-credit assignments. By asking the students to limit their focus to an event or events that have occurred "in the past year," Chris now realizes the inherent trauma that rests within that time frame.

For many students, this time period can be a time of great turmoil and upheaval. For many students, their entrance into collegiate life marks a separation from the relative stability of their home lives. Another potential traumatic influence—as Chris quickly realized when he pieced together the theme of broken relationships—is that this time period may also mark a student's first serious romantic relationship. There is also the obvious traumatizing influence of losing touch with friends as each student attempts to forge a new path for her or his life that is no longer bound by geographic limitations.

These serve as only a few examples of the subjects that Chris has seen his students take up in their extra-credit assignments, but each one emphasizes the potentially destabilizing effect that this period of their lives can have on students. Thus, Chris continues to offer this extra-credit assignment for his Composition I classes so that the students can continue—if they choose—to use it as a safe space to try to come to terms with this tumultuous period of time in their lives.

Again, it must be stressed that exercises like this can be hazardous for students, and that teachers should be careful not to force students to recall traumatic memories. Following the warning that is detailed earlier in this chapter, students must only write about their traumatic memories if *they* are the ones who suggest the idea, if they are not still currently exposed to the same traumatizing danger, if they feel they are ready to face the traumatic memories, and if they are encouraged to do so while they are under the supervision of a mental health care professional.

Another possible, though potentially challenging, approach is to situate trauma within a course theme. When Chris saw how students in his Composition I classes utilized assignments that had no obvious connections to trauma in order to attempt to work through traumatic events in their lives, it inspired him to make the bold (and possibly foolish, if it didn't work) decision to combine his research interest in trauma studies with his Composition II class to formulate a course theme of "pain and trauma."

Chris constructed the theme of the course so that, again, he was not forcing students to write about trauma in general or their own trauma specifically. He incorporated the subject of "pain" into the course theme so that students could avoid writing about trauma if they did not have traumatic experience that was applicable or if they wished to avoid facing a traumatic experience.

He also made the decision to scaffold his assignments so that most of the assignments for the course build toward the final research project. This means that he devotes early assignments in the course to proposing a topic that they would like to research, and to writing an annotated bibliography, which allows him to keep abreast of the progress his students are making in their projects. While this approach would, at first, seem to exclude the use of narratives in order to focus exclusively on research-based assignments, he has still left several of his assignments open to possibly include narratives.

The first essay that students write for Chris's Composition II class focusing on pain and trauma is a research proposal (see textbox 2.3). For this assignment, the students must incorporate two main pieces of information into their essays: (1) what they already know about the topic they would like to pursue for their final research papers, and (2) what questions they have about the topic that they would like to research. This approach allows students to write about their own experiences with the topic (if they choose to) when they are describing what they know about the topic.

TEXTBOX 2.3. UNIT 1: RESEARCH PROPOSAL

Context: In *Academic Research and Writing*, Linda S. Bergmann (2009) explains that "A proposal is written to persuade a specific reader or group of readers to accept a project before the major research is begun or while it is in its early stages" (p. 77). Thus, the research proposal is the foundation for a longer research project. In the research proposal, the writer has not yet had a chance to embark on the process of gathering information for the argumentative research paper. This means that the writer's idea will be in the early phases of development. While this will somewhat help to relieve the writer's stress, because it does not require the writer to have a fully developed idea just yet, the writer must still have taken a broad idea and narrowed it down to a more specific focus.

To illustrate how important it is for the writer to narrow down a broad idea to a more specific focus for the research proposal, let's look at an example of a broad idea and how to narrow it down. If the writer were to decide to pursue "coffee" as a broad idea, then you can see how this idea is still too broad. The ultimate goal for this class is to produce an argumentative research paper, which means that the author will make a persuasive argument about a specific topic. There may be thousands of ideas under the broad idea of "coffee" that the author could choose to pursue for the argumentative research paper. Thus, the audience that the writer is targeting in the research proposal would not have a very clear idea of what the focus of the essay would be if the writer used "coffee" as the topic for either the research proposal or the research paper. Instead, the writer must take this broad idea and narrow it down to something that she or he could eventually make an argument about, so that the audience for the research paper proposal can see where this idea could go.

So, the writer may narrow down the idea to "effects of coffee on house cats." Notice that the writer has narrowed down the broad topic, but is not yet making an argument. The argument will come later, in the argumentative research paper, after the writer has done enough research on the topic so that she or he can support the argument with the information gathered. At this point, though, it is easy for the audience of the research proposal paper to see that the writer could end up arguing that coffee has either positive or negative effects on house cats. However, at this point, this argument is still off in the writer's distant plans for this paper.

Assignment: Write a three- to four-page research proposal essay for an academic audience in which you propose a narrowed-down topic relating to the course theme of pain and trauma that you would like to research for your argumentative research paper.

In order to write this essay, you need not have started the researching process. Instead, you will focus on proposing a focused idea that you think you could pursue as a research topic as the thesis statement for the research proposal. This style of writing generally asks the writer to evaluate what she or he already knows about this topic as the starting point of the essay, in the first body paragraph. The writer then moves on to unresolved questions concerning the topic that she or he would like to use as research questions while researching the topic. Finally, the conclusion of the research proposal essay anticipates the objections of the audience and refutes those objections.

Please note that I will be either approving or denying your request to pursue this topic based on this essay. Thus, you may have to revise your approach to this topic based on my comments in this paper. If you are asked to revise your proposal or if you decide on a new topic, it is your responsibility to meet with me during office hours as soon as possible to receive approval.

Audience: Academic. This means that you should write in a style that is appropriate for this audience.

Format: This essay should be double-spaced, in Times New Roman font, and at least three pages in length. Please pay careful attention to the formatting guidelines provided in the course syllabus/policy sheet. Please note that you must print out a copy of the Unit 1 rubric and staple it to the end of the paper. If the rubric is not included, it will result in a 10 percent deduction from the grade for this essay.

Another approach that Chris uses in his Composition II course to allow students to explore traumatic experience through narratives involves a memorial essay that he assigns for their third unit. For the first two units in the class, students must choose a topic (the research proposal in unit 1) and present their research findings on that topic (the annotated bibliography in unit 2).

For unit 3, though, Chris decided to break from having students submit process work leading to their research papers in order to give them time to do extra research or to start drafting, and instead chose to focus this unit on healing from cultural traumas through memorials. Thus, for this paper (see textbox 2.4), Chris asks his students to pair up for group presentations. The two partners will then choose a cultural trauma that does not currently have a memorial devoted to it.[4]

TEXTBOX 2.4. UNIT 3: MEMORIAL ESSAY AND PRESENTATION

Context: It's difficult to classify the genre of writing that you will employ for your unit 3 essay. Because this unit involves partnering with others in the class, it means that each person in the group will be responsible for writing his or her section of the presentation as the essay that must be submitted for Unit 3. Thus, one person in the group will be tasked with writing a history of the event/person that is the focal point of the essay/presentation, and analyzing why this person/event is indicative of a cultural trauma to which we keep returning. The other member of the group must then present the design for the memorial, and explain why it is an appropriate representation for this memorial.

Assignment: Each group is responsible for first selecting an event/person that is somehow connected to the traumatic. This event/person must have no current memorial or monument devoted to it/him/her. Because each group member has a specific part to play in writing the paper and in delivering the presentation, I will describe each member's responsibilities in detail here:

> *Group member 1:* This person is responsible for delivering a seven- to ten-minute presentation that gives historical information about the event/person, and frames the event/person as something that is connected to the traumatic and to which we compulsively return. In doing so, it is important to keep in mind what the other member of the group will be covering in his or her presentation, so that you do not stray into your partner's area. Rather, you should keep your section focused specifically on the historical aspect of the event/person and why it is a cultural trauma. You are also responsible for writing a five- to six-page essay on this subject, but you should not just read this paper as part of your presentation.

Group member 2: This person is responsible for delivering a seven- to ten-minute presentation detailing the design of this memorial and explaining how it matches thematically with the event/person's connection to the traumatic. It would help tremendously if this group member has a creative background and is comfortable with either drawing by hand or digitally rendering materials. It is also important to keep in mind what the other member of the group will be covering in his or her presentation so that you do not stray into your partner's area. Rather, you should keep your section focused specifically on the design aspect of the memorial. You are also responsible for writing a five- to six-page essay on this subject, but you should not just read this paper as part of your presentation.

Each group presentation will last a total of 14–20 minutes, so it is essential that you practice this presentation as a group. Each group member is responsible for utilizing a minimum of three scholarly sources in his or her portion of the presentation and in the submitted paper, but both members of the group may use the same source(s). Each partner is also responsible for developing a visual aid (either a PowerPoint or a Prezi) to use during her or his presentation.

Audience: Academic. This means that you should write in a style that is appropriate for this audience.

Format: The essay should be formatted according to the guidelines provided in the course syllabus/policy sheet, and it must be a minimum of five pages. Please note that you must print out a copy of the unit 3 rubric and staple it to the end of the paper. If the rubric is not included, it will result in a 10 percent deduction from the grade for this essay.

Each group member is responsible for his or her own portion of the presentation. One is asked to explain the historical information related to the event and how this event qualifies as a cultural trauma, and the other is responsible for designing a memorial that is fitting for this cultural trauma. Here the process for designing the memorial is key for focusing on narratives.

In designing the memorial, the students are really designing a counternarrative to the narrative of the cultural trauma. In direct opposition to the narrative of the cultural trauma that claims that a population's communal identity is still marked by the trauma, a counternarrative instead argues for a path toward healing if the trauma can be properly memorialized.

For instance, in response to the sinking of the MV *Sewol*—the South Korean ferry that sank on April 16, 2014, killing more than 300 people—one group of Chris's students designed a memorial that included a wall with 304 holes carved into it (the exact number of people that perished in the accident), from which one drop of water would "weep" from each of the holes over the span of a minute to symbolize the loss of each person. This memorial demonstrates how powerful the narrative function is in this assignment. The memorial features two elements that are integral to forming a counternarrative to the narrative of the cultural trauma: the sense of loss (the "tears" to remind the viewer of the loss) and strength (the wall that symbolizes the endurance to move beyond the loss).

This is only one example of many elegantly designed counternarratives that Chris's students have submitted for this assignment. While it is different in nature compared to the other narratives Chris incorporates into his FYC courses because of its focus on cultural rather than personal experience, the assignment still follows the same basic framework that he has established in working with traumatic narratives.

Chris allows his students to choose the cultural trauma they want to work with for this unit, rather than assigning them a cultural trauma. This means that he is not forcing them to write about a cultural trauma that they might feel they have experienced. The students are free to write about a cultural trauma they have experienced if they choose, but Chris is conscious of the fact that his students could consider themselves part of a cultural trauma and may either be unable or unwilling to focus on an event to which they may have a deep connection.

Handled responsibly, it is possible to use narratives in first-year composition courses to give students an avenue for exploring traumatic experiences. While there is a fair amount of effort that must be made to provide students with safe spaces to explore these issues, the results, should they choose to do so, can be extraordinary for both the teacher and the student. By making narrative assignments accessible for writing about trauma, but not mandating such writing, we can give our students a powerful opportunity to bear witness if they feel they are ready to do so.

NOTES

1. This chapter examines topics such as sexual assault, which some readers may find disturbing. In cases where students are referenced, attempts have been made to protect their identities, and the authors have secured their permission to refer to them in this chapter.
2. While this reaction was involuntary, a reflex response born from a desire not to see someone else in pain, it is also good practice for dealing with an outcry from a survivor.
3. While the term "repression" surely has a problematic and unstable history as a psychological process, the term is used consciously here based on the work of psychiatrists Bessel O. van der Kolk and Otto van der Hart, who have shown that during a trauma the amygdala—the

section of the brain responsible for governing emotions—is active, while the cerebral cortex—the section of the brain responsible for constructing meaning—is not. This means that during a trauma, an individual may not be able to process what is occurring, giving us a biological process by which "repression" occurs. For a more complete discussion, see van der Kolk and van der Hart (1995).

4. For his definition of the term "cultural trauma," Chris utilizes Jeffrey C. Alexander's concept of the cultural trauma as something that is not naturally occurring, and which arises out of the desire of what Alexander terms "carrier groups" to frame the event as a trauma for a certain population. Thus, according to Alexander, cultural trauma is a socially constructed process, and Chris asks his students to consider if memorials work as socially constructed answers to a cultural trauma that allow the population to work through the trauma. For a more complete explanation of cultural trauma and carrier groups, see Alexander (2004).

REFERENCES

Alexander, J. C. (2004). Toward a theory of cultural trauma. In J. C. Alexander, R. Eyerman, B. Giesen, N. Smelser, & P. Sztompka (Eds.), *Cultural trauma and collective identity* (pp. 1–30). Berkeley, CA: University of California Press.

Bergman, L. S. (2009). *Academic research and writing: Inquiry and argument in college.* Boston: Longman.

Corkery, C. (2005). Literacy narratives and confidence building in the writing classroom. *Journal of Basic Writing, 24*(1), 48–67.

Goggin, P. N., & Goggin, M. D. (2006). Presence in absence: Discourses and teaching (in, on, and about) trauma. In Shane Borrowman (Ed.), *Trauma and the teaching of writing* (pp. 29–52). Albany, NY: State University of New York Press.

LaCapra, D. (2001). *Writing history, writing trauma.* Baltimore, MD: Johns Hopkins University Press.

LaCapra, D. (2004). *History in transit: Experience, identity, critical theory.* Ithaca, NY: Cornell University Press.

LaCapra, D. (2009). *History and its limits: Human, animal, violence.* Ithaca, NY: Cornell University Press.

Laub, D. (1995). Truth and testimony: The process and the struggle. In Cathy Caruth (Ed.), *Trauma: Explorations in memory* (pp. 61–75). Baltimore, MD: Johns Hopkins University Press.

Soliday, M. (1994). Translating self and difference through literacy narratives. *College English, 56*(5), 511.

van der Kolk, B. A., & van der Hart, O. (1995). The intrusive past: The flexibility of memory and the engraving of trauma. In Cathy Caruth (Ed.), *Trauma: Explorations in memory* (pp. 158–182). Baltimore, MD: Johns Hopkins University Press.

Chapter Three

Narratives as Gateways to Reflection

Courtney chuckled uncomfortably as she struggled to find an answer to the question. She pondered it seriously, rolling her eyes up toward the pocked ceiling as if to upload an appropriate response. The researcher, conducting a study on the use of reflective-based writing in courses outside of composition and writing studies, asked what challenges she faced in keeping a journal for her junior-level history course. Courtney cocked her head and stated, "Well, I thought it was only one page so that would not be a problem, but I don't really know why we're doing this."

When asked to elaborate on that last thought, Courtney pulled out two folded sheets of yellow notebook paper containing her first two journal entries. As the researcher looked at them, she added, "He [the instructor] said by the end of the semester, we will realize why he made us do the journal. But, now, I don't know. I'm just guessing. Do you know why we have to do the journals?"

Courtney's interview was part of a study Anthony conducted at Southern Illinois University–Carbondale in 2009–2010, as part of his dissertation research. The goal of the work was to gain more knowledge about students' reflective processes and the language that they use to describe reflective thought and action by focusing on multiple, discipline-specific contexts.

Exploratory in nature, the study focused on four writing-intensive courses within two disciplines—English and history—that regularly assigned reflective-based writing (journals, revision memos, reflective essays, etc.). Using interviews and textual analysis, the study examined the experiences of students reflecting on their own work within various course contexts.

Courtney, a senior history major at the time, enrolled in History 392 in the fall of 2009 and elected to participate in the research study. History 392 introduces students to research tools and methods used by professional historians to analyze and write history. The course is one of two required seminars for students majoring in history, history education, and related fields.

In the course, students composed an article-length (20–25 pages) research paper on a topic related to American history. As students developed their topics, researched primary and secondary sources, and engaged in scholarly exchanges with resource materials, they were required to track their progress in the journal. The journal was worth 10 percent of the final grade and was an informal assignment, as there are no penalties for grammar and spelling.

In outlining the assignment on the first day of class, the instructor, Professor Sweet, stipulated that their entries must be more specific than simple declarative statements, such as "I went to the library." Students were to use their journals to comment on what they have learned about history, ask questions, pose hypothetical scenarios about their research, discuss gaps in their knowledge, trace connections between their research and course concepts and personal experiences, reflect on what they have learned, and outline the work that still needs to be completed.

Courtney, as suggested by her interview responses, had a difficult time using the journal in this way. She speculated that she was to write about what she did each week but wanted to seek clarification from the professor on this point. While feeling uncertain about the overall purpose of the journal, she did not view it as being reflective in nature.

When asked to define "reflection" at the end of the interview, Courtney said that she only summarized her work from each week, implying that those summaries are not reflective.

To define the term, Courtney referenced her first-year composition course, which regularly assigned postwrites and reflective essays as part of the standardized syllabus. She stated, "Well, in my English class we had to do a paper and my teacher wanted me to write a reflection paper on that paper, like how I did it. In that way, reflection is probably like how you come to make that paper, or why did you produce that paper, or what did you think or whatever."

Shortly after the first research interview, Courtney dropped History 392.

EXPLORING REFLECTION AND REFLECTIVE WRITING

In a composition class, as students begin to produce essays that build on one another, perhaps in preparation for a writing portfolio or other culminating project, they will need to engage in a new kind of writing: reflection.

Composition students are often asked to reflect on their work, assessing their strengths and weaknesses, as well as their processes and habits. Reflective writing involves moving backward to review work that has been completed, and then often projecting forward to determine how the work can improved or revised.

However, developing the tools and language for engaging in deep reflection can be difficult for many students, particularly those new to academic writing. Maintaining an objective perspective can be challenging, particularly right after a student has completed an essay.

MacGregor (1993) suggested that beginning student writers "generally remain uncertain of how to write evaluatively about themselves, particularly in the absence of explicit examples or criteria of successful work in the class" (p. 38). Experienced student writers, she adds, may regard self-evaluative writing as busy work, producing only vague generalities, fragmented comments, and surface-level assessments that "communicate limited passion or engagement with learning" (p. 38).

Furthermore, as Courtney's story suggests, students can often base their perceptions of reflection and reflective writing on past experiences. If students encounter conceptions of reflection that appear to be at odds with their previous understanding of the concept, they may, like Courtney, fail to see the purpose of an assignment. They may also utilize forms of reflective writing in ways that run counter to an instructor's expectations. Finally, as Courtney discovered, instructors' conceptions of reflection may not always be fully defined or articulated.

Thus, this chapter focuses on reflection and the kinds of reflective writing that Courtney struggled to understand. It argues that stories and narratives can open new paths to reflection. Many students are comfortable with stories and narratives, which can ease tensions and concerns with reflection. Ultimately, embedding stories and narratives within written reflections can lead to deeper reflection and analysis.

First, this chapter will sketch an operational definition for "reflection" and "reflective writing" that will underscore specific strategies and recommendations proposed later. Second, it will explore discipline-specific research on reflection, emphasizing the role of stories in facilitating meaningful reflection. The next section will draw on these discussions to offer tangible ways to use stories and narratives to prompt student reflections. Finally, this chapter will conclude with implications for teachers.

THE DUAL DEMANDS OF REFLECTION

Reflective writing in composition comes in many forms and bears many names, including journals, postwrites, portfolio reflections, in-class reflections, and double-entry notebooks. While chapter 5 focuses specifically on portfolios and portfolio reflections, this chapter will explore shorter reflective texts, like journal entries and postwrites.

These kinds of reflective genres aim, essentially, to open a direct channel between the writer and an external audience in order to foster an ongoing dialogue about students' work. The thrust, then, is both contemplative and communicative.

These forms of writing can be informal or formal writing assignments, and often invite students to step outside of their experiences to assess rhetorical demands (audience, purpose, context, and ethos) of course assignments, reflect on the construction of essays, detect and diagnose strengths and weaknesses in their writings, develop and justify future actions and revisions, evaluate their progress on major papers and projects, and reflect on their overall development.

According to Yancey (1998), for a text to be classified as "reflective," it should have a dual nature. A truly reflective text should contain writing that engages in reflection, but also must be able to spur reflective thought. A narrative or short writing, like a journal entry, that only summarizes work that has been completed is not reflective; it can facilitate contemplation after reading, perhaps, but the writing itself does not plunge into complexities and contradictions. As Yancey concludes, a reflective text "enables us to make sense" (p. 187).

The journal assignment from the aforementioned study can illustrate this dual nature. Despite dropping her course, Courtney was not alone in her frustration about the research journal assignment. While a majority of the 16 other history students in the study understood the purpose of the journal, they viewed the journal as only a partially reflective text.

To the instructor of the history courses, "reflection" and "reflective journals" carried negative connotations related to personal opinions, beliefs, and preferences that had little connection to scholarly inquiry. During his introduction to the course, Professor Sweet avoided the term "reflection," stressing that "I care more about REASONING than reflections." The journals, then, focused more on summarizing work completed and assessing the quality of that work.

For the students, the act of recording ideas, notes, and research findings was not a reflective act by itself, but it potentially could have spurred reflective thinking. In other words, as one student noted, the journal only prompted reflective thought, but did not record it. Another student was blunt, stating that the journal constituted more of "a chore" than "a real form of reflection." In one of her interviews, this student explained this position more thoroughly: "At the end of the day we, as students, have done our day's research of indexes, bibliographies, and information found in the chosen books representing the necessary facts for our research, and now we need to 'reflect' or think about what we think about the information that we have discovered." In this description, the act of reflection is facilitated by the document, but the genre itself, as a collection of information, did not engage in deep reflection.

This particular journal assignment aligned with the instructors' goals and philosophy and, indeed, served a practical purpose. However, for instructors who want to foster deep reflection, texts must exhibit this duality.

REFLECTION ACROSS THE CURRICULUM

How can students, particularly novice writers who are new to reflecting on their work, develop this kind of dual-natured reflection? This is a particularly relevant question, considering that stories and narratives would only produce one-sided reflections. Venturing outside of the composition classroom, discipline-specific scholarship on reflection provides insight into the ways that personal narratives can foster deep reflection.

Quantitative studies investigated whether reflective writing in discipline-specific contexts enhances learning and improves student performance. Qualitative studies, on the other hand, traced students' reflective processes and explored the distinct ways in which they shape genres of reflective writing in discipline-specific contexts.

Studies of reflective writing and students' reflective processes can be found in disciplines as diverse as art therapy (Deaver & McAuliffe, 2009), dental education (Tsang & Walsh, 2010), nursing education (Langley & Brown, 2010), pharmacology (Edwards, Cleland, Bailey, McLachlan, & McVey, 2009) and philosophy (North, 1987). These studies focused on a variety of student populations, ranging from middle school students (Fracareta & Phillips, 2000) to graduate students (McAteer & Dewhurst, 2010).

A number of recent studies highlighted the reflective processes of second language learners. Key examples include Stevens, Serap, and Yamashita's qualitative study of two international graduate students (2010), McKenzie and Fitzsimmons's account of Australian pre-service teachers working in Fiji (2010), and Chi's report on how 12 Taiwanese pre-service English teachers used reflection to further their teaching (2010).

In addition to studying diverse populations, researchers also explored unique genres that promote and facilitate reflective practice, such as a drawing-based reflective journal (Tokolahi, 2010) and subjective diaries that welcome rather than discourage personal thoughts and feelings (Bradbury-Jones, Hughes, Murphy, Parry, & Sutton, 2009).

While the history instructor in the aforementioned research study required a focus on research over personal anecdotes due to concerns about unrelated digressions, discipline-specific research often illustrated how reflective genres, particularly personal and narrative-based writings, can intersect directly with course goals and concepts. Essentially, this rich body of research has explored how personal narratives can help to facilitate texts that engage in deep reflection and prompt further contemplation.

Through "conceptual blockbusting," Bean's (2001, p. 10) term for the process of reshaping writing activities to meet specific goals, instructors and researchers can adapt unexpected genres in meaningful ways. Parkinson (2005), for instance, recounted her department's experiences with an "underused genre" in an elementary literacy methods practicum courses for education majors. Developing strong reflective strategies was a key goal of the course, as students were assigned to review and assess their experiences in the field.

However, Parkinson found that previous genres, including "quick writes" and double-entry journals, proved unsuccessful. Along with her colleagues, she adapted the genre of the "friendly letter," requesting that students in the field compose a letter to their instructor before returning to the classroom (p. 148). The students, she reported, produced more in-depth responses that demonstrated higher-order thinking. Moreover, students' reflections were "filled with emotion and compassion" as they addressed relevant topics (p. 148).

Coker and Scarboro's 1990 analysis of writing-to-learn genres in a sociology theory seminar and a sociology of religion course extended the argument that personal- and narrative-based reflections enhance and support, as opposed to detract from, more analytical writing. The authors observed, "Journals often are similar to diaries; they are places for private reflection and exploration" (p. 221). While the authors underscored this notion as a benefit, this observation can provide insight into the misconception that writing detracts from content.

The perceived similarities between journals and personal diaries may further the misconception that narratives and personal reflections detract from analyses of course content, as students only use these forms to express irrelevant personal opinions.

On the contrary, Coker and Scarboro (1990) revealed that focused freewriting and guided journals can foster a more nuanced analysis of course content. On the use of journals, they reported, "Students are showing earlier a more marked sophistication in delving into classical sociological theory," adding, "They are more willing to risk making interpretations and receiving criticisms in class, are working more closely with the texts they read, and are more willing to challenge each other, the instructor, and the sources they read" (p. 219). While the authors focused on upper-level courses in which students may be more intrinsically motivated and have higher self-efficacy, their discussion emphasized the notion that more narrative-based reflections can be integrated effectively with analyses of course concepts and content.

THE TALE OF A TEXT

As discipline-specific scholarship on reflection has advocated, stories and personal narratives embedded in reflective genres can engage students and align with course concepts. More importantly, these narratives can facilitate truly reflective texts. Using stories to foster substantial reflection can be a challenge, however.

Alexander (2015) noted that past scholarship is not always clear as to how reflection is achieved. Using talk-aloud and think-aloud protocols, Alexander conducted a study in which composition instructors read literacy narratives and highlighted structures that they considered reflective. Instructors found reflection in cause-and-effect statements, evaluation (of cause-and-effect statements), metaphoric language, and ideological critiques (anti-academic appeals or school-based critiques, literacy as a shared activity, and literacy as equating to success).

Alexander (2015) found that, while many instructors find ideological critiques to be reflective, the study suggested that logical, argumentative structures were seen as more reflective. These findings present implications for literacy narrative prompts, as well as invention exercises. Instructors should generate invention questions that "(1) generate a memory (story) and (2) analyze and evaluate the effects (reflection)" (p. 62). This recommendation applies not just to invention prompts for literacy narratives, but also to short reflective memos and postwrites on essays. While Alexander found that many literacy narrative prompts focused solely on "culling memories and remembering past events" (p. 62), many prompts for short, reflective postwrites often move directly and solely toward analysis.

Reflections that ask students to reflect on their writing in general or even on specific pieces of writing may produce vague, surface-level reflections, especially if students are asked to reflect on their writing as a broad, nebulous body. Students, specifically underprepared students, may not possess the tools to engage in the kinds of deep reflection that instructors expect.

Oftentimes, students are asked to relate or discuss completed work without telling the story of that work. Prompts can often push students toward deep reflection and analysis without allowing students to engage in stories that might open the gates to deeper contemplation. The story of a student's computer crashing the night before a deadline may seem like a digression or distraction, but in fact could lead to a much deeper discussion of the text and what could be improved for the next essay.

If students are expected to engage in the kind of reflection that Yancey (1998) advocated, they must be able to engage in the messiness of reflection. That involves stories about texts, computer crashes, personal problems, and other issues. Those stories, however seemingly irrelevant, could propel a reflective piece to the level of making meaning out of the meaningless.

For example, a writing prompt that reads: "Reflect on your writing process for this essay. What are the main strengths and weaknesses of this piece?" moves directly toward analysis. Engaging in causal and evaluative arguments immediately, without build-up, could be difficult for any writer, let alone a neophyte writer still struggling to understand logical and analytic structures.

However, as the discipline-specific research above indicated, infusing reflection with stories, personal narratives, and personal examples can yield results. Narratives or stories, which many students are more comfortable writing, may help to jump-start reflective processes. By telling the tale of a text, the stories behind its creation, students may find an entry point toward critical reflection.

This can be true for expert writers as well. A former department chair of Anthony's once divulged that when she struggled with the writing for a book project, she pretended to be on the National Public Radio (NPR) interview show *Fresh Air*, with Terry Gross, engaging in a story about how she developed the idea for the text. The articulation of this tale of the text spurred a more objective and critical analysis of the text, leading to further development of the ideas.

Thus, a writing prompt that reads: "Tell the story of writing this paper, from receiving the assignment prompt to generating ideas and writing the drafts. Where did things go right? Where did things go wrong? What can you learn from the choices that you made in writing this paper?" can provide an inroad to analysis. Moreover, introducing a narrative dimension to short writing prompts can create a low-pressure space for students to engage with their own writing and ideas.

The sample prompt above is just one way to fuse stories and analysis. If students are having difficulty engaging in the kind of reflective analysis that is required, teachers can explore the idea of telling the story of a text in more creative ways. These kinds of prompts can add creative flourishes to engage students, particularly those who are more comfortable with writing poems, stories, and diary entries.

Critics may argue that this approach is a form of trickery, fooling students by masking an assignment with a creative flourish. Perhaps, but creative methods and literary devices have been embedded in scholarly conversations about reflection for decades.

In "Teaching the Other Self: The Writer's First Reader," Murray (1982) used personification to build on cognitive theories of reviewing and monitoring, developed by cognitive theorists to forward the concept of the "other self." According to Murray, as writers move through processes of writing, they engage in reflective conversations with the other self, which regulates the writing process by reading the writer's work and acting as a critic. This other self essentially provides the writer with the distance to objectively view the work and assess what needs to be improved or changed. Thus, for Murray this form of reflection comes alive as a mapmaker, a critic, and a sympathetic "chap" who guides and supports the writer (p. 142).

Putting this theory into practice, teachers can use personification in similar ways. To tap into the "other self," students can project ahead and think about how they might view their work at a later time. Creatively, this idea draws from science fiction, in which characters write notes and letters to future (or past) versions of themselves. Theoretically, it helps to build students' skills at projecting. As Yancey (1998) suggested, reflection places reviewing and projecting in conversations that look ahead to work in the future. The short exercise in textbox 3.1 helps to facilitate that internal dialogue.

TEXTBOX 3.1. IN-CLASS WRITING: FIRST-DRAFT REFLECTION

Write a short letter (two to three paragraphs) to your future self. Think about yourself in three months, as you are heading into finals. Your future self is busy (and tired) and has limited time. Based on your analysis of this current draft, tell your future self what needs to be revised in this essay to get it ready for the writing portfolio project. What are the most pressing needs?

Extending this use of personification even further, another way to engage students in active reflection is to ask them to personify their work, to think of it as a character. If the essay walked into the cafeteria, where would it sit? What kind of personality would it have? Addressing these kinds of questions, students could create a detailed portrait of the essay as a character: its appearance, its personality, and the problems and issues it faces (see textbox 3.2). The analysis part can come in by asking students to then explain these characterizations.

TEXTBOX 3.2. IN-CLASS WRITING: FINAL-DRAFT REFLECTION

Now that we have completed the unit 2 cause-and-effect essay on the effects of technology on writing, reflect on the finished draft. Imagine your essay as a person, a character with thoughts, feelings, mood

> swings, and habits. It's someone in the cafeteria, figuring out where to sit. In a short piece (one or two paragraphs), respond to the following questions:
>
> - If your essay were a person, what kind of person would it be (optimistic, sarcastic, angry, confused, etc.)? Describe its appearance and personality.
> - Why would you describe the essay in this way? Explain your "person," using examples and ideas from the essay as support.

In addition to creative, narrative-based prompts for prewriting exercises, concrete objects can act as a catalyst, mediating narratives and reflection. Scholars have noted the potential of concrete objects to foster reflection-based writing. From his experience, Hillocks (2007) suggested that students can develop the specific language needed to develop successful narratives by writing about "unusual natural objects" (p. 11). Other scholars have explored the impact of fine arts, emphasizing that abstract paintings (Karkabi, Wald, & Castel, 2014) and clay (Bar-On, 2007) can foster reflective thought.

Indeed, concrete objects, as subjects for writing, can open a space where both narratives and reflection intersect. In this space, students can engage in thoughtful reflection, as well as practice crafting shorter narratives. In exercises where objects are used to facilitate concrete language and precision in writing, introducing narrative and reflective elements can enable students to comprehend the subject on a deeper level, particularly if the object is something unusual.

For example, in Anthony's composition classes, he often asks students to write about objects that he brings to class, prior to writing their end-of-semester final reflections. The exercise is part of a lesson on showing and telling. Students learn the difference between telling—simply saying that they developed as writers—and showing—using examples and evidence to illustrate their development. Writing about an object, in this context, helps students to utilize descriptive language and concrete adjectives that could be useful in showing.

However, introducing narrative elements to this kind of exercise can also provide practice with reflection. During an exercise in which students were asked to describe an unfamiliar object, one student used a narrative structure to make sense of her subject. The object was a small, oblong pillow in the shape of a hockey goalie. A looped string sewn into the top allowed the pillow to be hung or dangled. The pillow was soft but not big enough to be practical. The student, Meredith, struggled to describe the object in any tangible way.

After holding and squeezing the object for a moment, Meredith found a way into her description. She realized that this was the kind of object given as a prize at carnival or fair games, a reward for throwing baseballs at plastic milk bottles or popping darts with balloons.

Using a narrative structure, Meredith pictured herself at a crowded, noisy fair on a summer night. She told the story of seeing her favorite hockey team's logo dangling high above the counter and suddenly feeling a need to win the object. Playing game after game of pong toss, she finally won the coveted prize. Summing up many people's experiences with winning odd prizes at carnival games, she concluded, "Now that I got it, I don't want it!"

This familiar narrative allowed Meredith to move behind just listing adjectives to describe the object and frame it within a familiar, almost common experience. As Hillocks (2007) argued, it is a "myth" that concrete sensory details are produced by using many adjectives. In fact, he claimed that "the quality of concreteness, or specificity, derives from the imagery produced largely by nouns and verbs and the function words that hold them together" (p. 21). Through Meredith's story, focusing more on a place, people, and actions, the odd-shaped object made sense and became more concrete.

In effect, instead of a prompt that asks students to "describe the object in concrete detail," ask them to encounter the object within a story. For instance, the prompt "Write a short story, in which you encounter this object. Within your narrative, develop a way to describe the object for your readers," could allow students to understand their assigned object more effectively.

As opposed to simply describing an object in a vacuum, a narrative-based exercise mirrors the kinds of writing that students regularly practice in composition. Typically, writers describe articles, people, and places within a larger context for a specific purpose. The inclusion of narrative in this exercise allows students to create that context.

Overall, there are myriad ways to bring analysis-based reflection and narrative in dialogue with one another. This discussion illustrates that embedding stories not only facilitates deeper reflection and analysis, but also provides a space for building clarity and specificity in writing.

POTENTIAL CONCERNS AND IMPLICATIONS

Despite the many benefits, infusing narratives into reflective prewriting can create potential conflicts and ethical dilemmas for instructors. Honest and in-depth reflections could create points of tension between students and teachers. On this point, the literature issues a caution.

Boud (2001) posits that journals, for instance, could cause embarrassment in the case of personal entries, or even elicit negative reactions from the instructor. A negative assessment of classroom practice in a student journal, he explains, could affect how the teacher perceives that student and any future coursework. He adds that simply imagining or anticipating such reactions could block the reflective process.

Professor Sweet, the history professor in the previously mentioned research study on writing-intensive courses, highlighted this conflict. Posing a hypothetical situation, he claimed: "If the student admits or says something in their journal that is controversial or sensitive, an instructor is vulnerable. ('Did he/she downgrade my journal because it was terse, or because I said I chose my history-of-homosexuality topic because I am gay?' I can see such allegations brewing from journals. For that reason, I ask students to focus on their research only)."

In "Ethical Concerns Relating to Journal Writing," English (2001) argued that to avoid such conflicts, instructors must establish clear parameters for entries, outlining "what is required and what is acceptable" (p. 31). Reaching a mutual understanding at the outset can overcome any anxiety related to content, and facilitate a productive dialogue.

This may be less of a concern for writing that is done quickly for private reflection, and not collected or worth a substantial amount of course credit. However, for work that is collected and shared with peers, as the sources above attested, instructors should set clear boundaries for what is and is not considered appropriate for reflective writing. This could be done through more detailed instructions, of course, but also through language-building discussions and exercises that define "reflection" and related terms.

A second potential concern for instructors is digressions. Inviting personal stories and narratives opens the possibility that students may not only digress from the subject at hand, but reshape the reflective genre in ways that differ from the instructor's intentions and expectations.

Providing a perspective on this issue, North (1987) conducted a case study of 53 students in a writing-intensive introductory philosophy course in order to explore the unique and diverse ways that the students interpreted the assignment. The course assigned a philosophical journal to enable students to develop, articulate, and reflect on their personal philosophies on key issues.

In sharing his findings, North offered profiles of three students: Alyson, Yvette, and Mark. Alyson and Yvette, both first-year students, used their journals to grasp philosophical discourse, focusing on readings and ideas. The third participant, Mark, a senior enrolled in his third philosophy course, aggressively argued his positions on philosophical issues in what North calls one side of a "shouting match" (p. 287). Upon reading North's profiles of the three students, the philosophy instructor was disappointed, noting that these three students wrote against his expectations for the journal. North concluded his analysis with a profound warning to teachers: "[W]hile we may assign students to keep journals as a way to learn about our disciplines, they will decide what those journals will be" (p. 288). Indeed, students potentially can bend and shape reflective prompts to suit their unique learning goals and needs.

For example, the prompt in textbox 3.2 that invites students to personify their essay draft as a character is open to a number of interpretations. Some students will, as directed, personify the traits of the writing, imagining a clean and well-organized person or a disheveled and frantic person, to cite a few possible examples. Others may use a celebrity, fictional character, or historical figure to visualize their essay.

When Anthony first experimented with this prompt, many students focused not on the quality of the writing, but the topic. They used descriptors like "passionate advocate" and "an ethical person" taking the "right," or what they saw as the appropriate, stance on important social issues. While this unexpected turn did not yield much reflection on the current strengths and weakness of the writing, it did solidify the students' stance on their topics.

In addition to suiting certain needs, students may also adapt a genre to adhere to their own unique conceptions of reflection, or even to the form of reflection that they perceive to be underscoring an assignment. These acts of shaping, molding, and adapting can occur both consciously and subconsciously. As a result, students' methods of utilization can sometimes be at odds with an instructor's expectations or original intentions for an assignment, creating complications.

This prospect, North (1987) warns, may be difficult for some teachers to accept. Specific prompts and instructions, as well as explicit discussions about reflection and reflective writing, can help to keep students on track. However, in reflecting on their own writing, students need to wander around in their own writing and stories. Some digressions and unexpected turns can be useful for students.

CONCLUSION

Crafting reflective prompts can be delicate work; the right amount of specificity is needed to set some necessary boundaries while still allowing room for creativity and expression. Essentially, reflection is building a common path with many possible side trails that circle back. While some specific parameters and language-building exercises may be necessary, short reflective writings work best if students have room to explore and share their stories, even if those stories open an unforeseen path. Otherwise, they may be staring at the ceiling, questioning the necessity of reflection.

REFERENCES

Alexander, K. P. (2015). From story to analysis: Reflection and uptake in the literacy narrative assignment. *Composition Studies, 43*(2), 43–71.

Bar-On, T. (2007). A meeting with clay: Individual narratives, self-reflection, and action. *Psychology of Aesthetics, Creativity, and the Arts, 1*(4), 225–236.

Bean, J. C. (2001). *Engaging ideas.* San Francisco, CA: Jossey-Bass.

Boud, D. (2001). Using journal writing to enhance reflective practice. In L. M. English & M. A. Gillen (Eds.), *Promoting journal writing in adult education: New directions for adult and continuing education* (pp. 9–18). San Francisco, CA: Jossey-Bass.

Bradbury-Jones, C., Hughes, S. M., Murphy, W., Parry, L., & Sutton, J. (2009). A new way of reflecting in nursing: The Peshkin approach. *Journal of Advanced Nursing, 65*(11), 2485–2493.

Chi, F. M. (2010). Reflection as teaching inquiry: Examples from Taiwanese in-service teachers. *Reflective Practice, 11*(2), 171–183.

Coker, F. H., & Scarboro, F. (1990). Writing to learn in upper-division sociology courses: Two case studies. *Teaching Sociology, 18*(2), 218–222.

Deaver, S. P., & McAuliffe, G. (2009). Reflective visual journaling during art therapy and counseling internships: A qualitative study. *Reflective Practice, 10*(5), 615–632.

Edwards, R. M., Cleland, J., Bailey, K., McLachlan, S., & McVey, L. (2009). Pharmacist prescribers' written reflection on developing their consultation skills. *Reflective Practice, 10*(4), 437–450.

English, L. M. (2001). Ethical concerns relating to journal writing. In L. M. English & M. A. Gillen (Eds.), *Promoting journal writing in adult education: New directions for adult and continuing education* (pp. 27–35). San Francisco, CA: Jossey-Bass.

Fracareta, P., & Phillips, D. J. (2000). Working with a writer's notebook. *English Journal, 89*(6), 105–113.

Hillocks, G., Jr. (2007). *Narrative writing: Learning a new model for teaching.* Portsmouth, NH: Heinmann.

Karkabi, K., Wald, H. S., & Castel, O. C. (2014). The use of abstract paintings and narratives to foster reflective capacity in medical educators: A multinational faculty development workshop. *Med Humanit, 40,* 44–48. doi:10.1136/medhum-2013-010378

Langley, M., & Brown, S. (2010). Perceptions of the use of reflective learning journals in online graduate nursing education. *Nursing Education Perspectives, 31*(1), 12–17.

MacGregor, J. (1993). Learning self-evaluation: Challenges for students. In J. MacGregor (Ed.), *Student self-evaluation: Fostering reflective learning* (pp. 35–46). San Francisco, CA: Jossey-Bass.

McAteer, M., & Dewhurst, J. (2010). Just thinking about stuff: Reflective learning: Jane's story. *Reflective Practice, 11*(1), 33–43.

McKenzie, B., & Fitzsimmons, P. (2010). Optimising personal and professional reflection in a unique environment: Making sense of an overseas professional experience. *Reflective Practice, 11*(1), 45–56.

Murray, D. (1982). Teaching the other self: The writer's first reader. *College Composition and Communication, 33*(2), 140–147.

North, S. (1987). Writing in a philosophy class: Three case studies. In T. Fulwiler (Ed.), *The journal book* (pp. 278–288). Portsmouth, NH: Boynton/Cook.

Parkinson, D. D. (2005). Unexpected student reflections from an underused genre. *College Teaching, 53*(4), 147–151.

Stevens, D., Serap, E., & Yamashita, M. (2010). Mentoring through reflective journal writing: A qualitative study by a mentor/professor and two international graduate students. *Reflective Practice, 11*(3), 347–367.

Tokolahi, E. (2010). Case study: Development of a drawing-based journal to facilitate reflective Inquiry. *Reflective Practice, 11*(2), 157–170.

Tsang, A. K. L., & Walsh, L. J. (2010). Oral health students' perceptions of clinical reflective learning—Relevance to their development as evolving professionals. *European Journal of Education, 14*(2), 99–105.

Yancey, K. B. (1998). *Reflection in the writing classroom.* Logan, UT: Utah State University Press.

Chapter Four

Narratives as a Catalyst for Research

It's no secret that students struggle to feel connected to a project in which they have no personal investment. When teachers assign topics, it is anyone's guess which students will be interested. At best, you can hope to pique the interest of half the class, which means the other half of the class sees this new project as a chore and not as an opportunity to learn and explore. It is important to allow students to choose their own topics so that they feel ownership (and a sense of commitment) to their projects.

Even when students do choose their own topics, they often make choices based on the things they already know something about—which means that the opportunity to learn, explore, and stretch themselves is almost as limited as when they are assigned a topic they're not interested in. The key is to impress on students the importance of treating research as an opportunity to learn, not as the task of compiling sources to support information they believe they already know or understand.

This is a tall order. The semester is short. Often the project students are working on for a class is just one of several for that class, in addition to projects for other classes they are taking. But the reward is great. If they actually approach research as a learning opportunity, their writing is much richer, better informed, and—most importantly—students begin to see research as something more than collecting quotations to insert strategically into their essays.

One possible solution to this research challenge is to encourage students to use personal narratives for the basis of their research. Students choose a story they know well—hopefully one they are directly involved in, but if not, then at least a story they have heard multiple times so that they are well acquainted with it. By starting on familiar ground, students should feel more comfortable with the material, and the push to research will be more enjoyable.

I-SEARCH, AND HOW IT DIFFERS

This personal narrative idea isn't so different from an I-Search paper, because both encourage personal investment in the topic and result in a personally rewarding project. The main difference is that an I-Search paper produces a narrative that tells the story of the research (literally about the process and method of the research itself). This approach is different in that it is proposing to use the story to drive the research and, ultimately, to create a richer, more complex piece of writing.

When Ken Macrorie first suggested a new type of research paper in his *New York Times* op-ed piece on September 3, 1979, he was frustrated about the current textbooks used in classrooms. Macrorie believed the existing textbooks disguised the research (and the process) that went into producing the polished text that students were supposed to learn from. Macrorie's (1979) comments hinted at the beginnings of the I-Search paper: "True investigators are excited, sustained in their work not by instructions but by curiosity. I thought that if I could show students why and how reference works were created, they would learn the use of each one because they would realize what needs each one answers" (p. A15).

These ideas were formalized in Macrorie's *Searching Writing* (1984) and updated in his *The I-Search Paper* (1988). In these works, the project is spelled out clearly: Choose a topic that you are seriously interested in learning about, conduct research of all kinds (interviews, surveys, more traditional secondary research, etc.), continue researching beyond the point where you believe you have a conclusive answer, and finally write the "story" of your search.

For Macrorie, that story includes your search, what you learned, and your reflections on the search. The use of story here is intentional, because as Macrorie (1988) reminded readers, storytelling is "the most fundamental mode of human communication" (p. 98). The sincere excitement of students engaged with their topic is infectious, and others feel that excitement and want to be part of the story: "If you let a genuine need or desire grab you, you'll find people helping so much that you become embarrassed" (Macrorie, 1988, p. 66).

Not all topics lend themselves to such primary research, but if a student's topic does, he or she will find the process rewarding and it will make their final written project unique. Additionally, primary research reinforces critical thinking, as nearly all proponents of the I-Search paper confirm.[1] Whether using primary research or not, the use of narrative has additional benefits.

Foremost among these benefits is empowering the student to have some level of expertise about a topic. Sommers and Saltz (2004) conducted a study at Harvard involving 422 students over the course of 4 years, with 65 randomly chosen students to participate in a subsample; his subsample was the basis for the study. From this group, Sommers and Saltz received important insight into the struggles of freshman writers.

Among these insights, perhaps the most telling is a senior reflecting back on her work as a freshman writer. That student reported feeling "as if she were being asked 'to build a house without any tools'" (Sommers & Saltz, 2004, p. 131). The researchers used this revelation to discuss the complex nature and high expectations of freshman composition courses, but they fail to address the opportunity composition instructors have to empower students by encouraging them to write about the self—a topic about which the student is an expert.

Sommers and Saltz (2004) were also able to identify trends in freshman writing that are important to acknowledge. Because students feel unequipped to perform the tasks they are asked to accomplish, they resort to "their old habits and formulas" from high school and do not progress beyond those time-tested techniques (p. 134).

Finally, one of the other major takeaways from Sommers and Saltz (2004) is the need for a paradigm shift. That shift, as the authors identify it, is toward "writing that matters" (p. 139). They, and others, have identified that students react most strongly to writing that has a "real" audience and purpose. When somebody other than the instructor, and perhaps a few peer reviewers, is reading the student's work, the student puts more effort into the writing and feels more rewarded when it is accomplished. The lesson here is that it is important to shake students up and "trick" them into pushing their boundaries.

The I-Search paper is one way to push students to increase depth of content and their personal investment in topic selection; however, in the modern academic clime, more rigor is required. Therefore, a more effective approach is a method that borrows some of the tenets of the I-Search project and marries them with more academic demands. In the process, instructors can empower students to write about subjects they are familiar with, while challenging them to investigate a greater depth of content rather than simply finding evidence to support what they already know.

The basic idea is to use personal narrative as a catalyst for research and writing. By beginning on familiar ground, students feel comfortable with the subject matter, and because they are a part of the story, the research they conduct will be personally fulfilling. Through the research, they will better understand how their narrative fits into the historical context, as well as better understand the various references embedded in the story (many of which they have never stopped to consider).

An additional benefit of this method is that the story forms a frame and provides a consistent line for the finished writing. Anecdotes are a well-known successful method for introductions, and a student writing from his or her own narrative should be able to easily choose an anecdote to introduce and conclude his or her essay. Because the research begins and ultimately ends with the student's story, the story will provide cohesion to the finished writing.

THE STORY OF THE MOCK RAID

Michael frequently uses his own personal narratives in his classes, and the following "mock raid" story is one he has used for various reasons (sometimes for students to practice summary, other times to paint a picture of the late Cold War period that he grew up in, and still other times to inspire students to tell their own stories). Before he tells the tale, he explains that this story has been told many times and, as such stories do, has taken on a life of its own.

He explains that because stories morph and change over time, and because memory is fluid and subjective, it is essential to reevaluate the "truths" in any story, perhaps most importantly the stories you know best. Michael then tells a version of the story in textbox 4.1.

TEXTBOX 4.1. PERSONAL NARRATIVE: THE MOCK RAID

I grew up in a small town called Saline in the 1980s, during the Cold War. My friends and I were fixated on the idea of nuclear war and the military in general, so we owned M16 rifle–shaped BB guns, dressed in camouflage, and prepared for the assumed Russian invasion. Movies like *Red Dawn*, *War Games*, *Rambo*, and even *Spies Like Us* inspired and terrified us. My best friend, Paul, and I used to cull through the *Weekly Reader*, a Scholastic newspaper for kids, for interesting articles that we would then glue into notebooks. Not sure why we glued them into notebooks, because we never referred back to them, but that's what we did. One day, in 1985 or 1986, an article titled "The Mock Raid" caught our eye.

The story was about how the U.S. military was testing to see how prepared citizens were for a potential invasion. They conducted various mock raids throughout the country, but the one in this particular story was about invading a high school. The military, I don't remember which branch, hovered over the high school in black helicopters, and men rappelled down from them and invaded the high school. It should come as no surprise that the high school students and staff didn't know what to do, and so the article concluded that Americans are unprepared for an attack on U.S. soil. Paul and I then decided we needed to conduct our own mock raid.

For a short time, we considered raiding our elementary school, because it was in Paul's backyard, but ultimately we decided that the school was too big for a couple of kids to take on. We decided to raid one of our houses instead. We invited two other "Mikes" to be part of our raiding party. (I was one of nine Mikes at my school, so we went by last names; the two Mikes we invited were Hicks and Hahn.) My house was the obvious choice, because my parents were younger and cooler, and because it sat on a corner lot, providing us with two easy points of entry.

The plan was as follows: Saturday morning, I would leave my house, dressed in plainclothes, ensuring that the front and side doors were unlocked. Then I would meet my friends by a group of trees across the street where we had stashed our camouflage clothing, face paint, BB guns, smoke bombs, and other gear. After changing, we would head back across the street, Hicks and Paul would go to the front door, and Hahn and I would go to the side entrance. Paul had stolen his father's starter pistol, and Hicks would be armed with an unloaded BB gun. Hahn had my unloaded BB gun, and I would be equipped with smoke bombs glued to the bottom of a margarine tub. At the signal, Hahn would light the smoke bombs, I would open the door and slide the smoke bombs across the linoleum floor, and at the same time Paul and Hicks would enter the front door, firing their weapons before eventually grabbing my three-year-old brother, Ryan. Once completed, we would flee to the woods with my brother.

That was our initial plan. What really happened was a little different. My mother had noticed I'd left the side door unlocked, and had locked it on us. So, I had to knock on the door, and when she came to open it, I still tried to slide the margarine tub across the linoleum floor, but her knees got in the way. The tub of smoke bombs fell over and caught a rug on fire. I heard Paul and Hicks shout, "We got him," and we ran for the woods.

We let my brother go about 10 minutes after kidnapping him, but hid in the woods all day to delay our punishment. Eventually, we came home to face the music. Paul was grounded for taking his dad's starter pistol. Hahn was grounded because his family was close with Paul's family, and so the two were often grounded at the same time. Hicks was grounded because his mom was mean (at least, as children, we thought she was). I had to pay for the burned rug, but since my friends were grounded, I was effectively grounded as well.

This story has a text embedded within it—the initial article in the *Weekly Reader*. The quest for this document is what began Michael's research into his personal narrative. Though he was unable to locate that particular article, in the process of searching he was able to find several other national articles discussing similar mock raids. From these sources, he was able to determine more about the motivations of the mock raid that he read about when he was in sixth or seventh grade.

All the articles pointed to fears of Communist invasion and American readiness to fend off such attacks. This understanding then steered the research toward an exploration of Cold War politics and, eventually, to discussing the anxieties and fears that his family felt during the time of his friends' mock raid. Each discussion, or interview, sparked new research questions and prompted further investigation.

This particular project ultimately took the form of a multigenre research project composed of separate distinct pieces of writing, but it should be noted that those elements could have been integrated into a more traditional piece of research-based writing.

For the multigenre research project, Michael included the following sections: a definition of the Cold War, summaries of newspaper articles discussing the Communist threat, biographies of the participants of the mock raid, a map of the neighborhood (marked with the relevant locations), a retelling of the mock raid on the family home, recollections and memories of the other participants, and photocopies of newspaper accounts of mock raids around the country during the time of Michael's own mock raid.[2] Each of these shorter pieces was inspired by questions raised by the original narrative. Students asked, "What's the Cold War?" which prompted Michael to research the topic more thoroughly in order to give a concise and complete answer.

Similarly, students asked what the other people mentioned in the story remembered of the event. This, in turn, inspired Michael to ask his brother, friends, and mother about what they remembered. An inquiry on what the neighborhood looked like sent Michael into finding maps of his hometown from the 1980s so that he could reconstruct the streets and houses in his story. Each of these student questions pushed the storyteller to learn more about the elements of his story, which created a well-rounded, informed narrative.

Not every student's story is going to include an obvious opportunity to provide an objective, documented account as Michael's does, but even a simple story about a night with friends, a family reunion, or a T-ball game implicitly includes other parties with whom to consult. Each conversation may spark topics for research for greater understanding. Students will gain a better understanding of their own story by talking with others who participated in and observed the events. The more diverse (particularly in terms of age) the subjects interviewed, the better and richer the story will become.

BREAKING IT DOWN

It can be difficult for students to objectively see events that they are so familiar with (particularly stories they have told multiple times). It helps to provide prompts for students to break down a story into components. Textbox 4.2 lists are some prompts that can offer guidance for students with this project.

TEXTBOX 4.2. PROMPTS TO HELP STUDENTS RESEARCH THEIR NARRATIVES

- When did the story take place? It is important to be as specific as possible. Be sure to include day of the week, month, day, year, and time of day. If you don't, look them up, or ask someone. The online calendar timeanddate.com can be helpful in determining what days of the week for a specific month and year.
- Who participated in the story? If this were fiction, we would ask, "Who were the characters?" So, who are the characters? How old are they? How well do you know them? Where did they come from? What are their backgrounds? What is their relationship to you?
- Who observed this story? Essentially I'm asking for witnesses. And again, who are these people? How old are they? What are their backgrounds? What is their relationship to you?
- What else do you remember from this period of your life? Do you remember what was in the news? What was your favorite song? What was your favorite TV show? Who was your best friend? What was your favorite book?
- Have you told this story to anyone else? What was their reaction to it? Did this person know you when the story occurred? If so, did they correct you on any of the details or add anything to the story?
- If the events in your story were inspired by something, what inspired it?
- What happened after the story was over? Or, to ask another way, what was the aftermath?

Each of these questions is an opportunity for the students to research or verify elements of his or her story. The initial research may begin as primary research, with a conversation or an email, but then it is essential to find another objective source to validate the information discovered. By requiring this, the assignment reinforces the necessity of thorough and ethical research.

This method creates a scaffolding effect. Each conversation inspires research to verify or corroborate, and each new piece of information inspires a new conversation with peers. This new conversation in turn reveals new information, which requires further investigation and research.

Frequently, details that seem insignificant end up revealing tangential pieces of information of great import. For example, a favorite song or TV show can help pinpoint the time and date when an event actually occurred. In the case of Michael's story, he could not remember the exact year the mock raid took place, but by investigating other newspaper accounts, he was able to narrow those results to a three-year window. A conversation with each of his friends helped to further narrow the date, and his mother helped pinpoint the specific year and month when the story took place.

IMPLICATIONS

Humans have been telling stories for centuries, and it is natural to embrace storytelling in the classroom, but it is important to harness the power of narrative toward the course objectives. This is achievable by using a personal narrative as a jumping-off point for research. In addition to motivating students to perform primary and secondary research, sharing stories also has several other positive benefits.

A story helps form a sense of community in the classroom. Because students are sharing their stories with one another, students become invested in one another's stories and their projects. As a result, they inquire about one another's projects, and when they find information that might be relevant or helpful, they pass it on. Similarly, peer review goes more smoothly when the subject matter is a topic that students feel mastery over. Finally, because students are more interested in these topics, they take the peer review more seriously, and offer more insightful feedback on the writing and research.

While students do tend to be hesitant to make critical remarks about personal narratives (especially narratives that deal with sensitive subject matter), they are particularly helpful in other ways. Freshman writers often struggle with where to end a personal narrative, and their peers, as objective outsiders, can be helpful in this regard. Additionally, stories lend themselves to further investigation, as peer-review feedback often helps the writer identify important details that he or she may have overlooked.

In Michael's experience, questions and comments from peers (audience members) aren't seen as threatening, but instead are taken as inquiries from attentive listeners (or readers). In addition to helping students identify important details to include, information to expand on, or how to end a story, students should be encouraged to ask (and often do ask, without prompting) how aspects of the story fit in. This question helps reinforce the writing objective of overall unity in the project.

Finally, it is important to have discussions about the credibility of a storyteller. Students frequently tell stories that seem unbelievable, because those are typically the ones that are most memorable. Knowing that, it is vital for students to build credibility so that their audience does believe their stories and isn't constantly questioning the authenticity of the narratives. This is a perfect opportunity for discussion of logos, pathos, and ethos, and how a student can incorporate those elements into his or her writing and storytelling.

CONCLUSION

By providing students the opportunity to conduct research about a topic that they do feel mastery over (their own story), they are given the chance to succeed and enjoy the process. Investigating their own story takes some of the sting out of academic research and helps them to better understand why, how, and when to use sources.

Once their narrative-based research project is complete, students then should be encouraged to transfer these skills to another assignment where they are not as "personally invested" in the topic. The challenge then is for them to find a personal connection, however tenuous it might be, to this topic. It is through that personal investment that students will find reward in the research process. The narrative-based research project is simply a gateway to ease them to this point.

NOTES

1. See Appling-Jenson, Anzai, and Gonzalez (2014), Assaf, Ash, Saunders, and Johnson (2011), Feldbusch (2007), and Luther (2006), in addition to Macrorie (1988).

2. Michael has written more extensively about this in his collaboration with Heidi Burns, *Intellectual Creativity in First-Year Composition Classes* (2016).

REFERENCES

Appling-Jenson, B., Anzai, C., & Gonzalez, K. (2014). Bringing passion to the research process: The I-Search paper. In M. L. Warner (Ed.), *Teaching writing grades 7–12 in an era of assessment: Passion and practice* (pp. 130–152). Boston: Pearson.

Assaf, L. C., Ash, G. E., Saunders, J., & Johnson, J. (2011). Renewing two seminal literacy practices: I-Charts and I-Search papers. *Voices from the Middle, 18*(4), 31–42.

Burns, H. W., & MacBride, M. (2016). *Intellectual creativity in first-year composition classes.* Lanham, MD: Rowman & Littlefield.

Feldbusch, R. (2007). Seeing academic writing with a new "I." *National Writing Project.* January. Retrieved from http://www.nwp.org/cs/public/print/resource/2371

Luther, J. (2006). I-Searching in context: Thinking critically about the research unit. *English Journal, 95*(4), 68–74. doi:10.2307/30047092

Macrorie, K. (1979). Textbooks that don't embalm. *New York Times*, September 3, p. A15.

Macrorie, K. (1984, 1988). *The I-Search paper* (Revised edition of *Searching writing*). Portsmouth, NH: Boynton/Cook.

Sommers, N., & Saltz, L. (2004). The novice as expert: Writing the freshman year. *College Composition and Communication, 56*(1), 124–149. doi:10.2307/4140684

Chapter Five

As the Semester Ends

The Writing Portfolio as Narrative

"Not another one," Chris whispered to himself.

Chris had spent the entire day grading the final portfolios for his Composition I class, and he had been distressed to find the same recurring problem in many of the reflective introductions—the cover letters, assigned to introduce the portfolio to the audience, placed before the revised essays in the portfolio. The students were focusing far too much on grammar.

Chris had spent time in class patiently detailing what was supposed to be in the reflective introduction. He had told them that the reflective introduction acts as a companion piece to the portfolio. It would tell the reader how the student's writing process had changed over the course of the semester; the portfolio would demonstrate that change.

In his notes in class, Chris had explained how the changes in the students' writing processes could include elements like grammar and punctuation, but that he was far less concerned with lower-level issues like these. Instead, he preferred that students went into more detail explaining higher-level issues, such as attention to audience and to genre conventions. All of the students seemed to be attentively taking notes, and they asked questions that led Chris to believe that they were "getting it."

However, when he started grading the portfolios, he noticed one common theme. Reflective introduction after reflective introduction examined in great detail the lower-level issues while nearly completely ignoring the higher-level issues. It wasn't just one student; it was endemic to the entire class. Chris realized he had a problem.

The students, Chris surmised, had done what they thought they were *supposed* to do. He wanted them to talk about changes they had made in their writing processes, and they had literally written about changes they had made in their writing processes as they were preparing their final portfolios. However, Chris could hardly blame them for taking his instructions so literally, despite the detailed notes in class telling them not to do exactly what they did, because he realized it was his fault.

When Chris, like most experienced teachers, sees an error that appears as a recurring error across a large sampling of his students' work, he doesn't automatically jump to the conclusion that they are all poor writers, and that they should drop out of college at once and get jobs as animal caretakers at their local zoos. Instead, he internalizes the error and reflects on his practices in organizing the information for the class and disseminating that information to the students. In other words, he tries to figure out how he screwed up.

In this instance, he was pretty sure he knew what he did wrong. Chris typically likes to utilize process work after a major essay assignment is submitted to allow students to reflect on their efforts in the work they have just submitted. He has found that a process assignment like a postwrite that asks students to reflect on the strengths and the weaknesses of a work can be invaluable in directing students to focus on higher-level issues rather than lower-level issues, because they do not have the draft right in front of them to find those lower-level issues. Instead, they are forced to recall their macro, or "big picture," approach to constructing the essay.

Chris then asks the students to keep track of these process assignments to utilize when they are drafting their reflective introductions. He tells the students that they will not receive a grade for the process assignments until they submit them at the end of the semester with their portfolios. While he may have one or two students who lose their postwrites each semester, most of the students diligently keep track of these process assignments so that they do not miss out on that grade.

However, Chris skipped the process work this time. His ability to reflect on his approach to teaching this assignment led him to a valuable insight that is probably correct. Skipping the postwrites probably did hinder his ability to convey to the students how they should approach the portfolio assignment. And there is one other area that Chris missed that also could have helped to convey the main goals of the assignment: a metaphor that would allow students to visualize the assignment in order to better understand it.

This chapter focuses on the writing portfolio—more specifically, the reflective introduction or cover letter for the portfolio—as a narrative of the changes that have taken place in a student's writing process. Reframing the reflective introduction as a narrative may allow students to more fully understand the role of the portfolio and to take ownership of the finished product. Moreover, this chapter builds on chapter 3, which explores the intersections between stories and short reflective assignments, to emphasize the importance of informal, process-based assignments in shaping portfolio narratives.

PLACEMENT PORTFOLIOS

Before we turn our attention to the writing portfolio typically seen in FYC courses, we must first acknowledge students may already be familiar with the general concept of portfolios before they enter the composition classroom. Students may have been asked to assemble art portfolios, or they may have heard of investment portfolios. They may have already started their own, or they may have been asked by a potential employer to provide them with an application portfolio. Wherever they picked up the term, they may already be familiar with the concept of the portfolio as a collection of their work.

One usage of the portfolio concept that students may be familiar with before taking a composition course is the placement portfolio. Placement portfolios have gained popularity in recent years as writing program administrators (WPAs) search for fairer and more expedient ways to place students in composition courses. Placement portfolios may also be used by administrators to allow students to challenge their placement in a particular composition course according to standardized test scores.

In assessing the placement portfolio, it is essential that the students' needs and best interests be kept in mind at all times. This is acknowledged in the Conference on College Composition and Communication's (CCCC) "Writing Assessment: A Position Statement" (2014), which claimed: "Decision-makers should carefully weigh the educational costs and benefits of timed tests, portfolios, directed self-placement, etc. In the minds of those assessed, each of these methods implicitly establishes its value over that of others, so the first impact is likely to be on what students come to believe about writing" (n.p.).

Thus, when placing students in a composition course, administrators need to carefully consider how students may perceive the evaluation method compared to other placement methods. In the case of portfolio placement, CCCC contended that "the value of portfolio assessment is that it honors the processes by which writers develop their ideas and re-negotiate how their communications are heard within a language community" (n.p.).

Portfolio placement, then, is something that students value as a process that is similar to the recursive writing process most FYC teachers champion; however, it is important that students are given the chance to participate in the process of evaluating their portfolios, in addition to the compilation and submission of the portfolios. As CCCC claimed, "Students should have the right to weigh in on their assessment" (n.p.). This means that, while the student should not have the final decision on how the portfolio is assessed, she or he should be allowed to offer an opinion on the quality of the portfolio before the assessment, and then to respond to the decision following the assessment.

The student's feedback in the portfolio placement process is invaluable because of what comes next. If the assessment determines that the student may not be placed in her or his desired composition class, then the logical outcome for the student will be to enroll in the course into which that student has been placed.[1] If the student has not been permitted to respond to the determination and to feel like her or his opinions on the process are valued, then it could potentially lead to that student's resistance to the material in the course and the teacher who is presenting the material, which could hinder the student's progress.

Thus, a student in an FYC classroom may already be familiar with portfolios from going through a portfolio placement at the college or university. If so, and if the student was permitted to respond to the assessment of her or his work in the portfolio, then this student may already have an understanding of how portfolios work. It would then be up to the individual instructor of the FYC course to demonstrate for the student, as we demonstrate later in this chapter, how the portfolio can be visualized as a narrative, and how the placement portfolio can act as a "prequel."

THE ARGUMENT FOR PORTFOLIOS AS NARRATIVES

This chapter makes two major arguments concerning the use of portfolios in FYC classes: (1) that portfolios can be an invaluable resource for assessing and encouraging growth in students' writing habits, and (2) that instructors can encourage students to visualize portfolios as narratives in order to allow students to more easily understand and engage with the process of constructing a portfolio.

The first argument—that portfolios can perform a vital function within a FYC class—is hardly as controversial as it once was. The field has come quite a way from Elbow and Belanoff's (1986) contention that "[t]he portfolio system makes some teachers feel a bit uncomfortable—especially the first time they use it" (p. 337). Portfolios now are widely accepted, and even those instructors who choose not to use them would likely concede that they do operate in much the way that Elbow and Belanoff envision them to, as a way of encouraging "revising, peer feedback, and collaboration among students" (p. 337).

The widespread acceptance of portfolio usage in an FYC classroom does not come without some reservations, though. For instance, Elbow (1994) provided some valuable warnings to proponents of portfolios, cautioning them against the very system he helped to popularize. Elbow warned against the dangers of holistic scoring and overassessment. These are hardly the only objections to portfolios, as others have pointed out the potential for grade inflation (Neal, 1998) and possible increases in plagiarism when used at the programmatic level (Schuster, 1994).

However, these objections are usually met with proposed solutions rather than a general dismissal of the use of portfolios, which further reinforces their value despite some real or perceived flaws. This chapter does not take issue with the general acceptance of portfolios, but proposes a creative reconceptualization of portfolios and how they are presented to students. Visualizing the portfolio as a narrative—as a chronological process—can better help to prepare students to compile portfolios.

While there is some deviation from this pattern, the writing portfolio has some recurring elements to its composition. Elbow (1994) described the portfolio as "multiple pieces of writing, written on multiple occasions, in multiple genres, directed to different audiences, written in more or less realistic writing conditions" (p. 44).

One of the genres that is frequently included in the writing portfolio is the cover letter or the reflective introduction to the portfolio.[2] As Conway (1994) claimed, "The cover letter is probably the most consistently required document appearing in students' writing portfolios" (p. 83). Elbow (1994) called the cover letter "one of the most important and useful documents in most portfolios" (p. 41). Thus, the cover letter is generally an indispensable part of the portfolio.

The cover letter is such a vital part of the process of compiling a portfolio because of the role it plays in reflection. Elbow (1994) explained, "The student must explain and reflect on what is in the portfolio and talk about processes used in writing the pieces and putting the portfolio together. The cover letter helps students become more thoughtful and aware about their writing processes—helping them with metathinking and metadiscourse" (p. 41).

Conway (1994) clarified that portfolios are "expected not only to show the documents students have written, but also to tell something about the people who wrote them," and that the cover letter is the desired venue for this type of exposition (p. 83).

If the cover letter or reflective introduction is so important for conveying student identity, then it is necessary to find a proper way to ask students to envision this document to convey this knowledge. In Conway's (1994) examination of cover letters, she preferred to refer to them as "masks." She claimed that, in asking students to reflect on changes in their writing processes, instructors are really asking students if they "knew some of what it means to think like academic writers" (p. 85).

However, past attempts to describe the proper way to visualize the cover letter have proved to be an awkward fit. For instance, Conway conceded, "It may well be that such knowledge is really only a mask adopted for the purposes of writing a strong cover letter" (p. 85). Conway's metaphor of the mask, then, is really a critique of students' abilities to grasp and engage in academic discourse. Students appropriate the mask in an attempt to mimic academic discourse, but this language points out that this approach is inherently disposable; the mask can be discarded once the assignment is completed, with the possibility of never wearing it again.

A better fit for understanding the role that the reflective introduction plays in the portfolio is to encourage students to envision it—the portfolio as a whole, but specifically the reflective introduction—as a narrative, a story they are telling about themselves. This metaphor seems to be already ingrained in our thinking about reflective introductions. Instructors are asking students to reflect on an event that happened to them in order to suss out its importance or its deeper meaning. It is typically told in chronological order. It contains a plot, characters, and settings. All of these are genre conventions of a narrative.

If students can understand the reflective introduction as a story they are telling about themselves—about how their writing processes have changed over the course of this class—and they can see the other documents in the portfolio as demonstrations of those changes (to follow the metaphor being developed here, as illustrations or photographs that appear in their stories to help the reader visualize the details)—then we believe that this approach will introduce students to a better and more lasting understanding of the role that reflection plays in shaping their writing processes.

SETTING THE SCENE: DESCRIBING PORTFOLIOS IN COURSE DOCUMENTS

Although some students may enter an FYC classroom with a general understanding of the concept of portfolios, the instructor still needs to anticipate that not all students will have been introduced to this concept, and may need a patient, guided introduction to the concept and a description of how the portfolio will operate in this specific class so as to standardize everyone's approach to preparing a portfolio.

The concept of the portfolio and how it should be assembled can be explained at the very start of the course by providing a description in the course syllabus. For example, Chris's syllabus for a Composition I class contains such a description:

> This class utilizes a portfolio system, which is a collection of student work. This means that you are responsible for keeping the graded copies of the major essay assignments once they are graded and returned to you, so that you may make revisions and resubmit them in the portfolio at the end of the semester. The purpose of a portfolio is for students to track the changes in their writing as the semester progresses—to tell the story of their growth as writers. The

changes that we will focus on for this class are changes in content, addressing genre conventions (the rules for each style of writing), and grammar and mechanics. At the end of the semester, you will be required to submit the original graded drafts and revised drafts of the major essays, along with a reflection on how your writing has changed over the course of this semester, in a portfolio. The completed portfolio, then, will tell your reader a story about how your writing has changed in the reflective piece, and then it will demonstrate the changes in the revisions you have made to the essays.

Chris is careful to provide five key elements in this description:

1. A general explanation of the concept of a portfolio as "a collection of student work"
2. An explanation of the purpose of the portfolio—"to track the changes in their writing as the semester progresses"
3. A description of the changes he wants students to focus on—"changes in content, addressing genre conventions (the rules for each style of writing), and grammar and mechanics"
4. An introduction to the directions for compiling the portfolio, which requires "the original graded drafts and revised drafts of the major essays, along with a reflection on how [the student's] writing has changed over the course of this semester"
5. The metaphor equating the concept of the reflective introduction and the portfolio with a narrative, to allow students to visualize it.

Each element is essential in preparing students to complete the portfolio. The students must understand the underlying rationale for why they are being asked to perform this task—as is the case with most tasks performed in the composition classroom—and they must understand how to compile the assignment and what the instructor's expectations are for this assignment. Instructors are encouraged to return to these elements often throughout the course of the class, and to prepare supplemental materials, such as an assignment prompt for the portfolio, to reinforce the goals of this assignment.

THE PLOT: THE ROLE OF INFORMAL ASSIGNMENTS IN BUILDING THE STORY

To follow this metaphor of the reflective introduction and portfolio as a story of the growth of a student's writing process, there is one final element to address: the role of informal assignments. As discussed in chapter 3, informal reflective assignments can be crafted in specific ways to incorporate narrative elements. Thus, informal assignments like prewrites, postwrites, journal exercises, drafts, peer reviews, notes, assignments from the textbook, and all of the other process work that instructors do on a daily basis can be visualized as the plot of the story.

The plot of a story involves the actions that happen to and around the character(s) throughout the course of a narrative. If there is a character who is the protagonist (the student), and who experiences events (the daily activities) in a class, then a plot can take shape.

This device allows students more autonomy and creativity in drafting their reflective introductions. Is the student a protagonist who decided her own fate through the efforts she has taken to revise her work this semester? Does the student feel that she has been the unwitting pawn of the machinations of a malevolent villain (you, the instructor who has graded her work, or the technology, the dreaded adversary who deleted all of her work when her computer crashed)?

Rather than mimicking academic discourse as suggested in Conway's conceptualization of the mask, the concept of the narrative with a plot allows the student to proceed in more than one direction, and to do so organically, based on the student's perceptions of her or his own efforts. This approach could potentially help lead students to focus more on higher-level aspects of those efforts.

CONCLUSION

Returning to Chris's story at the beginning of this chapter, his efforts to teach students how the portfolio system worked were hindered because he chose not to include the postwrites as part of the process work he assigned throughout the semester. He felt that without that process work, the students could not clearly understand the expectations for this assignment.

If Chris had used the metaphor argued for here, then he could have framed the postwrites as an integral part of the plot that was missing. In Chris's experience, the students focused on grammar in their reflective introductions because that is their perception of what polished academic writing looks like—it is the mask that they appropriated.

However, if Chris had used the metaphor of the portfolio as a narrative—starting with the design of course documents framing it in this way, emphasizing this metaphor with informal assignments comprising the plot, and then underscoring the reflective introduction and the portfolio at the end of the class as the vehicle for conveying the narrative and visually depicting details of the narrative—this approach could have allowed his students to better visualize and understand the concept of the portfolio on a deeper level.

NOTES

1. While this may not necessarily be the next step for the student, as she or he could attempt to further appeal the decision with other administrators at the college or university, the process is simplified here to cut to the logical end point in the process so as not to get lost in digressions that try to anticipate the nearly endless permutations of appeals possibilities that depend on the individual campus and its unique administrative hierarchy.

2. "Reflective introduction" is the preferred term here to describe this document, as it has a deeper resonance in visualizing the portfolio as a narrative than the term "cover letter."

REFERENCES

Conference on College Composition and Communication. (2014). *Writing assessment: A position statement*. Retrieved from http://www.ncte.org/cccc/resources/positions/writingassessment

Conway, G. (1994). Portfolio cover letters, students' self-presentation, and teachers' ethics. In L. Black, D. A. Daiker, J. Sommers, & G. Stygall (Eds.), *New directions in portfolio assessment* (pp. 83–92). Portsmouth, NH: Boynton/Cook.

Elbow, P. (1994). Will the virtues of portfolios blind us to their potential dangers? In L. Black, D. A. Daiker, J. Sommers, & G. Stygall (Eds.), *New directions in portfolio assessment* (pp. 40–55). Portsmouth, NH: Boynton/Cook.

Elbow, P., & Belanoff, P. (1986). Portfolios as a substitute for proficiency examinations. *College Composition and Communication, 37*(3), 336–339.

Neal, M. (1998). The politics and perils of portfolio grading. In F. Zak & C. C. Weaver (Eds.), *The theory and practice of grading writing: Problems and possibilities,* (pp. 123–138). Albany, NY: State University of New York Press.

Schuster, C. I. (1994). Climbing the slippery slope of assessment: The programmatic use of writing portfolios. In L. Black, D. A. Daiker, J. Sommers, & G. Stygall (Eds.), *New directions in portfolio assessment* (pp. 314–324). Portsmouth, NH: Boynton/Cook.

Chapter Six

Stories in an Online Environment

One of the most important challenges of teaching in an online environment is creating a sense of community and a space similar to the physical classroom. Most online classes encourage students to write a short biography as a means of introduction.[1] These biographies, or personal narratives, serve to introduce students to their classmates.

The objective is for students to find commonalities among classmates in the hope that those similarities will begin conversations and form relationships. Students can bond over similar experiences, just as they do in a traditional classroom setting. In many ways, the "personal biography" serves as the first impression for students in an online environment.

Although it is possible to upload a profile picture to the learning management system used by the class (such as Desire2Learn, Moodle, Blackboard, and others), it is uncommon to require students to provide profile pictures. Left to their own devices, students frequently ignore this option. This leaves the student biography, or introduction, as the sole "first impression" for students. And, of course, first impressions are important, and a bad first impression is notably difficult to overcome.

THE DESIRE FOR AN ONLINE COMMUNITY

The desire to create a community in the online classroom is born out of a few basic understandings. First, students are more willing to share when they feel comfortable with, and know more about, the individuals they are sharing with. Sharing pays dividends in the form of students participating in discussion, wanting to impress their peers with their writing, and providing a diverse set of perspectives in the classroom.

Second, a sense of community makes group work and peer review easier. Finally, and perhaps the most pressing concern for institutions with online courses, a sense of community makes students feel responsible to the community, which in turns makes them less likely to disappear from the course.

Simply put, community increases retention, and retention is a serious issue for online classes. Depending on the study, retention rates for students in online classes range from 10 percent to 50 percent lower than in face-to-face classes (though between 10 and 20 percent is a generally accepted figure).[2] While the various studies argue about what else might help with retention, all agree that a sense of "community" helps students feel connected to the class.

As Drouin (2008) has pointed out, the biggest deficit in students' sense of "community" in an online setting is the perceived inability to "communicate with their classmates" (p. 277). It is essential to encourage students to communicate with one another to overcome this obstacle, especially since most students take composition courses in their first year when they are also most likely to withdraw from or fail an online course.[3]

Sanders, Daly, and Fitzgerald (2016) conducted a study with 198 first-year university students to investigate attrition rates. In their conclusion, the authors reinforced Trawler (as cited in Sanders et al., 2016), stating that "engagement is a prerequisite of success" (p. 75). The easiest way to get students to feel "engaged" is to create a sense of community. Typically, a sense of community in a traditional classroom begins to emerge from intentional icebreakers during the first week of class.[4]

That type of community, however, raises superficial connections and relies on the hope that students will have common experiences that allow them to bond. A more lasting sense of connection can be generated by encouraging students to work together to meet a common objective. It is important to structure the activity carefully, because just as collaboration can result in a lasting positive connection, failed collaboration can result in a lasting desire to not work together again.

Ku, Tseng, and Akarasriworn (2013) conducted a study of 197 graduate students in distance-learning classes that required group work. Their study showed that the groups that reported higher "team dynamics" also reported higher teamwork satisfaction. Students felt the greatest level of satisfaction when they were able to effectively communicate student-to-student. While it's easy to say that the technology makes it easy for students to communicate with one another, it is difficult to motivate students to use the technology to speak with one another.

BUILDING "ANONYMOUS" GROUPS

Such collaborations can prove fruitful, but they can be difficult for instructors in composition courses. Typically, the online education model has been sold as an individual endeavor at a student's own pace. Collaboration flies in the face of that. However, in a traditional classroom, collaboration is encouraged in the form of informal classroom activities and discussion. It is strange that while online education attempts to re-create the classroom in so many ways, collaboration is not frequently attempted, nor successful.

The answer to successful online collaboration, and community building, is to encourage similar collaborations in the online environment and to allow students to form relationships with one another through the coursework rather than through an introductory biography. By delaying the "reveal" of difference, students will learn to value one another's opinions and to overcome initial biases. Through discussion, differences will be revealed, but much more gradually. Further, this will occur after students have already given one another the benefit of the doubt about being more like themselves than different, and have discovered other similarities.

For this reason, it essential to let students know that the collaborative assignment will be graded, and that it is worth a substantial number of points. The "stick" method (in lieu of the "carrot"), in addition to assigning a creative activity, should motivate participation. Because this activity happens at the beginning of the semester, it should help form good habits and result in a greater sense of community, respect for collaborative projects, and familiarity with the technology available to communicate with one another. See textbox 6.1 for one example of an activity.

TEXTBOX 6.1. A COLLABORATIVE ASSIGNMENT FOR STUDENTS TAKING AN ONLINE COMPOSITION COURSE

Objectives: Encourage students to collaborate, become more comfortable with editing one another's work, instill a sense of how the writing process works, and ensure familiarity the course syllabus. By the end of this activity, students should be able to:

- Understand the expectations, assignments, responsibilities, and texts of the course
- Perform light research, prewrite, draft, edit, and revise written work
- Provide thoughtful and critical feedback to their peers
- Be more comfortable with group dynamics and collaboration

Approximate time required: 75–120 minutes

Materials needed: course syllabus

Rationale: Simply put, collaboration is difficult, and students don't typically like "group work." Yet the very thing that students dislike, or at least feel uncomfortable with, is the key to making them feel part of a community in a classroom. In an online environment that classroom becomes much more ambiguous, and the need for collaboration is even greater. By directing students to perform research about the class syllabus, they benefit from learning about course policies, expectations, assignments, and texts. Having students then share that information with one another reinforces their learning. Finally, making them collaborate with one another and edit each other's work not only performs a "double-check" (to ensure they have grasped the concepts), but also pushes students out of their comfort zone and forces them to depend on one another.

What to do during class: Students should be randomly assigned to groups of three or four. Most learning management systems offer a group function and the opportunity to randomize group members, which makes this task easy. Each group will produce an informative newsletter about the class. The objective is to educate one another about the class in which they all find themselves. Of course, the syllabus does this, but a newsletter written by their peers will be more interesting to read, and perhaps more approachable.

Each member will be assigned one of the following roles: content generator, editor, format/layout. If groups have more than three, extra members should be assigned the role of content generator. The content generator's responsibility is to write. The editor's responsibility is to make decisions about what content will go into the newsletter, and what revisions are necessary. The format/layout member is responsible for choosing the font, deciding on the layout of the newsletter, and making decisions on such questions as whether images will be used, or if the newsletter will have a name or title.

Because it's important that each student participate in each of the roles, they should alternate turns. Each student will create content for the newsletter, each student will edit one another's work, and each student will have say in layout decisions. However, the student who is assigned a particular role has the final say. As a group, the students need to decide which topics they will touch on. The instructor can assign topics to be mandatory content, or leave this up to the students.

> Students should be empowered to make decisions regarding their own newsletter, because this is a student newsletter for the other students, and a supplement to the already existing course syllabus.
>
> **What to do following the activity**: If in an online class, have the students post their newsletters in a discussion forum with an accompanying introduction that explains the rhetorical choices they made on what to include in the newsletter and how to best present that information. If in a traditional classroom, have students print enough newsletters to go around, and discuss their rhetorical choices in an informal presentation.
>
> As a larger group (or larger discussion forum), hold a discussion about what material was most important to include in the newsletters, how the team worked as a group, what issues arose with the process, and any other reflective comments about the activity. Finally, answer any questions about the syllabus that remain after the newsletters have been shared and read.

This activity was devised with the four guiding principles for collaboration as outlined by Abrami, Bernard, Bures, Borokhovski, and Tamin (2011):

1. Structure positive interdependence such that one student's success positively influences the chances of other students' successes.
2. Highlight individual accountability so that each student is responsible for his or her own learning, and helping the other group members learn.
3. Ensure that promotive interactions occur by allowing individuals to encourage and facilitate each other's efforts to accomplish the group's goals.
4. Maximize the likelihood that students give and receive elaborate explanations with a focus on encouraging understanding in others. (p. 99)

When done well, these guidelines help offset most students' hesitation regarding "group work." While on the surface a newsletter-type assignment may not seem very difficult, it has several of the suggestions made by Abrami et al. (2011) built into it. The very nature of a newsroom, with a pool of editors, content generators, and layout designers, requires both collaboration and individuality at all stages. By having students review, or peer review/edit, one another's work, they learn from what another student has written, thus reinforcing their own knowledge of the content and grammatical rules by reading and interviewing another student's work.

With an assignment like this, the hope is that students will be able to flex both their independent and group muscles, and learn to work with one another. By requiring collaboration early in the course—in the first week especially—an important tone is set and an expectation is established. This is especially vital in an online class. It provides a relatively low-stakes opportunity for collaboration and encourages students to become familiar with one another's strengths without the need for students to disclose information about themselves.

This anonymity prevents students from forming cliques with one another based on common experiences or interests, and instead encourages collaboration regardless of interest, gender, or other identifying attributes. This is an opportunity that only the online classroom provides. It would be extremely difficult to re-create a similar environment in a face-to-face classroom setting, and so it is important to take advantage of this unique opportunity.

Joinson's "Self-disclosure in Computer-mediated Communication" (2001) offered particularly telling information about the possibilities of anonymity. In his review of the literature, Joinson summarizes Reingold (1993): "New, meaningful relationships can be formed in cyberspace because of, not despite, its limitations" (p. 178). Reingold believed that the Internet will "be a place where people often end up revealing themselves far more intimately than they would be inclined to do without the intermediation of screens and pseudonyms" (as cited in Joinson, 2001, p. 179).

The fact that people are willing to engage with unknown users is one that can be harnessed in the online environment. Joinson (2001) further remarked that "under the protective cloak of anonymity users can express the way they truly feel and think" (p. 179). This willingness to express oneself, and the increased confidence to do so, means that a student who might otherwise be a quiet group member can make his or her thoughts known.

In collaboration, it is especially important that all voices are heard, and that all participants are happy with the work that is produced. Again, this is another strength of online collaboration. But it is important that this collaboration is modeled early in the semester and its importance to student success in the class is impressed on each student. Once those relationships are formed, they are easy for students to return to, but establishing them is difficult once an alternative pattern or expectation has been set.

Similarly, once students have disclosed information about themselves (or shared images), it is difficult to overcome those superficial obstacles. This, again, is why it is important to begin the class with anonymous collaboration. Prior to sharing images or disclosing information, Internet users assume other users are like themselves until they prove themselves otherwise. Every piece of information disclosed is another layer of difference to separate them. If we can moderate this disclosure, or at least minimize or delay it, the hope is that more fruitful and lasting collaborations and relationships can be formed.

REMOVING THE RESTRICTIONS, AND SHARING

It is only natural that, through any communication, students will begin to see differences among one another. Rather than continue to fight disclosure once the initial collaboration is completed, it is best to embrace the more traditional route of student biography, or personal narrative. It is important to take a couple of steps to ensure this transition is effective.

In order to successfully use stories in any classroom setting, it is important to give students the tools that allow them to properly respond to sensitive material. While the "stranger on a train" phenomenon can be used successfully to get students to "open up," it also means that students will frequently confess instances of abuse, addiction, and other similarly sensitive topics. While these can be powerful opportunities for students to process their experiences, it is very difficult for their peers to constructively respond.

For students revealing this information, these are indeed defining moments that make them who they are, and these are the things that they include in their biographies. Rather than sparking conversation, these confessions frequently elicit responses such as "I'm so sorry to hear this," or no response at all. At times, students who have experienced similar situations may chime in and use the opportunity to commiserate and recount their own experiences.

While these moments can be fruitful in terms of forming a sort of "support group," they often derail the discussion and fail to provide the type of "community" that was intended. Instead, students feel more isolated because of the difference that is disclosed, and are more cautious about engaging those students in classroom discussion. Further, English instructors are not formally trained to handle some of the traumatic experiences that a student may reveal, which leaves the student particularly vulnerable after opening up emotionally.

The essential tool that all students need is the ability to focus on the writing, and not the subject. But this is a difficult thing to teach students to do with their peers. The key is to start with an unknown entity (a subject outside of the class) and to have them analyze that writing before engaging with sensitive writing from their classmates.

An easy way to accomplish this is to have the instructor provide a writing sample that he or she has written (or writes specifically for this class).[5] Students often feel freer to criticize a work without the fear of offending the author, and so it is recommended that the authorship not be disclosed until after the discussion has concluded. Often the first comments students make will be about the "story" that is told, but they should be encouraged to look beyond the narrative and examine the work more critically in terms of form, style, cohesion, and other elements.

Of course, the point in having students write a biography is to allow them the opportunity to tell the class who they are, but this is also an opportunity to focus on "real" writing with a "real" audience. The message to get across to students is that they can do both: reveal information about themselves, and write clearly, cohesively, and effectively.

Using a narrative, or biography, written by the instructor has additional benefits. First, as discussed earlier in chapter 1, self-disclosure by the instructor can help the student feel more connected to the class by seeing the instructor as something beyond an authority figure. Second, most students who are given an example before being asked to write something of their own will use that example as a model. Because the instructor is producing this biography or narrative for the class, he or she has opportunity to model what the student should produce, and can talk about the pitfalls or struggles he or she experienced while producing the short piece.

Once the class has successfully navigated responding to personal narratives provided by the instructor, they should be instructed to create their own narratives. Though it may seem to be common sense, it bears repeating to students that what they wish to disclose about themselves it is up to them. Simply because it happened to them, does not mean they need to tell it. Further, just like any other piece of writing, their personal narrative should have a thesis and a clear focus, not simply a list of occurrences or dates or a timeline.

CONCLUSION

Teaching in the online environment has its difficulties, but the hope is that this chapter has exposed the way to take advantage of the unique opportunity provided in the online classroom. By harnessing the shield of anonymity and delaying the exposure of the inevitable differences among students, it is hoped that collaboration will be easier and will help students overcome the superficial differences made obvious in a traditional classroom. Stories can be used, and should be used, but not before students get to know one another through collaboration and writing.

It is important to note that difference and exposure to alternative perspectives (cultural or otherwise) is an essential trait of a liberal education. This is one way in which the anonymity of online education falls short. But, that same anonymity can also inspire collaborations between students who, in a traditional classroom, would resist partnering with one another. In this way, the Internet bridges a divide that is otherwise difficult to cross.

NOTES

1. The Conference on College Composition and Communication's "A Position Statement of Principles and Example Effective Practices for Online Writing Instruction" (2013, March) provides several suggestions for best practices. Principle 11 is most relevant to the discussion of student introductions: "Online writing teachers and their institutions should develop personalized and interpersonal online communities to foster student success" (n.p.). After issuing the principle, there are several examples offered, including "teachers should develop course community early by employing 'icebreakers' and other activities that make use of the LMS and that engage student writing"; "informal student writing integrated in the course (e.g., asynchronous discussions, blogs, reading responses) should use the technological opportunities that most likely will elicit meaningful responses among class participants"; and "teachers should develop forums, threads, and assessments in which students can have open discussions, either with or without teacher involvement, about course dynamics" (n.p.).
2. See the introduction to Glazier (2016), "Building Rapport to Improve Retention and Success in Online Classes," for a succinct summary of the various studies about retention rates.
3. See Cochran, Campbell, Baker, and Leads (2014), "The Role of Student Characteristics in Predicting Retention in Online Courses" (p. 42).
4. See chapter 1 in this book.
5. Of course, there are plenty of professionally written short biographical pieces, or personal narratives, or creative nonfiction, that could be used for this activity as well.

REFERENCES

Abrami, P. C., Bernard, R. M., Bures, E. M., Borokhovski, E., & Tamin, R. (2011). Interaction in distance education and online learning: Using evidence and theory to improve practice. *Journal of Computing in Higher Education 23*, 82–103. doi:10.1007/s12528-011-9043-x

Cochran, J. D., Campbell, S. M., Baker, H. M., & Leads, E. M. (2014). The role of student characteristics in predicting retention in online courses. *Research in Higher Education, 55*, 27–48. doi:10.1007s11162-013-9305-8

Conference on College Composition and Communication. (2013, March). *A position statement of principles and example effective practices for online writing instruction*. Retrieved from http://www.ncte.org/cccc/resources/positions/owiprinciples

Drouin, M. A. (2008). The relationship between students' perceived sense of community and satisfaction, achievement, and retention in an online course. *Quarterly Review of Distance Education, 9*(3), 267–284.

Glazier, R. A. (2016). Building rapport to improve retention and success in online classes. *Journal of Political Science Education, 12*(4), 1–20. doi:10.1080/15512169.2016.1155994

Joinson, A. N. (2001). Self-disclosure in computer mediated communication: The role of self-awareness and visual anonymity. *European Journal of Social Psychology 31*(2): 177–192. doi:10.1002/ejsp.36

Ku, H.-Y., Tseng, H. W., & Akarasriworn, C. (2013). Collaboration factors, teamwork satisfaction, and student attitudes toward online collaborative learning. *Computers in Human Behavior, 29*(3), 922–929. doi:10.1016/j.chb.2012.12.019

Sanders, L., Daly, A. P., & Fitzgerald, K. (2016). Predicting retention, understanding attrition: A prospective study of foundation year students. *Widening Participation and Lifelong Learning, 16*(2), 50–75. doi:10.5456/WPLL.18.2.50

Part II

Implications and Conclusions

Chapter Seven

"Why Did You Give *Me* Such a Bad Grade?"

Providing Constructive Assessment of Narratives

Once Chris had handed back all of the narratives, he noticed one student hanging back as the other students from the class trickled out of the room. This wasn't unusual, of course, as students often stuck around after class, especially after papers were graded and handed back, to ask questions.

However, this case was different, as this student was typically quiet in class, preferring to remain silent when the rest of the class engaged in class discussions or group activities. Furthermore, Chris recalled that the grade the student had earned on this assignment wasn't particularly bad.

The student, a male in his late teens or early twenties, appeared to be gathering his thoughts as Chris continued packing up his belongings and turning off the technology in the classroom. It was clear that the student was nervous about approaching Chris, and he didn't want to make the student feel even more pressure by asking him what he wanted before he was ready.

After a minute or so, the student finally approached Chris to ask him if they could set up a time to meet to discuss the feedback on his paper. Chris has a 24-hour rule for meeting with students to discuss their papers when they have been handed back. In other words, he asks students to wait 24 hours after essays have been returned before meeting with them about the comments on their papers or the grade, so that they take the time to review the comments after the initial shock of the grade has worn off. Thus, the student asked Chris if they could schedule a meeting for the next day.

When the student arrived for his meeting the next day at Chris's office, it was clear that he was still lost in thought about the paper. He was quiet and reserved, and when Chris asked him what he could do to help him, the student first asked a procedural question about an upcoming assignment, which was an obvious attempt to stall, before finally leading in to his real reason for the meeting.

"Why did you give me such a bad grade on this assignment?" the student asked.

Chris responded by asking the student to retrieve the essay from his backpack and to turn to the comments at the end of the essay. Chris carefully guided the student through each end comment and how the essay's performance was assessed, before turning his attention to explaining his comments in the margins of the paper. He concluded by explaining that a "B" wasn't really a "bad grade."

The student frowned and replied, "No, that's not what I meant. Why did you give *me* such a bad grade?"

From the emphasis on the word "me," Chris finally understood why the student was so displeased by his grade.

Narratives, by their very nature, are personal. A narrative requires the writer/storyteller to pass the story through a filter of his or her own perceptions, feelings, and experiences in order to narrate the story.

For this student, this assignment was not just a set of skills that he was trying to learn to achieve mastery of the outcomes for the course. Instead, the process of writing this narrative was a deeply personal process that led the student to believe that he, personally, was being assessed, rather than the quality of his work.

This instance illustrates one of the most pressing issues in assessing narratives. Due to the personal nature of the writing assignment, the narrative assignment can lead to students feeling that their personal identity is being assessed as much as the assignment itself. This is why it is necessary to have a comprehensive approach to assessing narratives.

After reflecting on the earlier scene, Chris realized that he had made several mistakes in his assessment methods for this essay. He had given the students an assignment prompt and several weeks of lessons to help guide them in completing the narrative, but he had not provided them with a rubric to help guide them in drafting the essay and in interpreting his comments on the graded copy of the essay.

This chapter contends that in assessing students' narratives, it is essential for instructors to provide two pieces of feedback: (1) a clear and concise rubric that the students have an opportunity to review before they complete the assignment, and (2) formative comments at the end of the essay that form a narrative.

RUBRICS AS AN EXTENSION OF NARRATIVE

Rubrics are generally accepted as a reliable assessment measure when grading student work. As Goodrich (1996) clarified, "A rubric is a scoring tool that lists the criteria for a piece of work, or 'what counts' (for example, purpose, organization, details, voice, and mechanics are often what count in a piece of writing); it also articulates gradations of quality for each criterion from excellent to poor" (p. 14).

Here, Goodrich defined the typical rubric. While she acknowledged, "The term defies a dictionary definition" (p. 14), she did provide an invaluable starting point in understanding what a rubric is, and how it is used. A rubric is generally a listing of the criteria for assessing an essay, and those criteria are usually arranged in grid form to make it easier to read and understand. However, Goodrich is missing a valuable clarification: that there are different types of rubrics.

Two main types of rubrics are employed for assessing writing, and each style of rubric has its own function. Arter and McTighe (2001) defined holistic rubrics as giving "a single score or rating for an entire product or performance based on an overall impression of a student's work. In essence, one combines all the important ingredients of a performance or product to arrive at an overall, single judgement of quality" (p. 18). Textbox 7.1 is an example of a holistic rubric.

TEXTBOX 7.1. SAMPLE HOLISTIC RUBRIC

Level 2: Demonstrates a below-average use of many of the following elements of a narrative:

- A logical and coherent order for the events in the narrative, such as a chronological order
- Understanding of important characteristics of a narrative, such as plot, characterization, and setting
- Dialogue as a valuable method to convey exposition of the plot
- [Other criteria as outlined by the instructor]

Level 1: Does not achieve any of the following elements of a narrative:

- A logical and coherent order for the events in the narrative, such as a chronological order

---

- Understanding of important characteristics of a narrative, such as plot, characterization, and setting
- Dialogue as a valuable method to convey exposition of the plot
- [Other criteria as outlined by the instructor]

This textbox demonstrates some of the common characteristics of a holistic rubric. Each "level" provides a means to assess the main characteristics of the assignment. Beneath each level are the formal criteria that are being used to assess the assignment.

The other main type of rubric for assessing writing is the analytical rubric. Arter and McTighe (2001) defined the analytical rubric as dividing a "product or performance into essential traits or dimensions so that they can be judged separately—one analyzes a product or performance for essential traits. A separate score is provided for each trait" (p. 18). Table 7.1 is an example of an analytical rubric.

The table illustrates the major traits of the analytical rubric. One line along the top provides the different levels of execution. Then, each characteristic is provided along the side so that the assessor can evaluate each characteristic according to the level.

The choice as to which rubric to use is up to the instructor of the class; however, the analytical rubric seems to be more in line with the strategies offered in this chapter and this book. Arter and McTighe (2001) clarified that one drawback to using a holistic rubric is that "there is no detailed analysis of the strengths and weaknesses of a product or performance" (p. 21).

However, the analytical rubric is useful for overcoming this specific weakness in holistic rubrics. Arter and McTighe (2001) contended that analytical rubrics provide "more specific information or feedback to students, parents, and teachers about the strengths and weaknesses of a performance. Teachers can use the information provided by analytic evaluation to target instruction to particular areas of need" (p. 22).

Thus, while both holistic and analytical rubrics can be constructed and used effectively to assess writing assignments, the analytical rubric allows for instructors to provide more specific feedback. More specific feedback, in the case of assessing narratives, is ideal because it allows an instructor to clarify that she or he is assessing how well the narrative utilizes features of the narrative genre, rather than allow students to mistakenly believe that the instructor is assessing their personal experiences.

Table 7.1. Sample Analytical Rubric

	Excellent	Above Average	Average	Below Average	Deficient
	Essay is highly successful in this area, possessing few if any errors	Essay exceeds expectations in this area, possessing only a few errors	Essay possesses some errors in this area	Essay possesses numerous errors in this area	Essay demonstrates a lack of understanding of this area
1. *Purpose:* Essay has a clear purpose					
2. *Structure:* Essay contains a logical and coherent organization that adheres to the genre conventions of the assigned genre of writing					

USING FORMATIVE COMMENTARY: FEEDBACK AS NARRATIVE

Before moving on to the use of formative commentary as a narrative while assessing narratives, it is first necessary to distinguish between summative and formative commentary. Summative commentary is offered as evaluative feedback at the end of the student's learning process. Liu (2013) contended that summative feedback "is the assessment focusing on the final results when certain teaching activity comes to an end" (p. 2188).

In contrast, formative assessment evaluates student progress while it is going on, to allow students to adjust. As Liu (2013) argued, "Formative assessment evaluates the efficacy of the teaching activity itself during the process of teaching in order to adjust the process of activity and to ensure that the goals of the instruction are being achieved" (p. 2187).

The difference between summative and formative commentary, though, can be slippery. As Ussher and Earl (2010) claimed,

> It is not the test or teacher-made resource or assessment task that is summative or formative, rather it is how you use the information gathered through such activities. Or, to put it another way, it is the meaning made from the results of the assessment and the consequences (decisions and actions) resulting from the meanings rather than the assessment task itself. Clearly, one task can be used for a variety of purposes. (p. 60)

Thus, the task itself does not define whether the commentary is formative or summative. That distinction is made by the instructor when she or he decides how the feedback should be used by the students. This chapter, then, utilizes formative feedback as the term to describe the feedback the instructor provides at the end of the comments, as this book as a whole approaches revision as an integral part of the recursive writing process.[1]

In drafting these formative comments, adding one final step can help to emphasize that the instructor is assessing the work rather than the student's personal experiences. Instructors can use narrative commentary in their formative comments in order to emphasize that their critique is aimed at the assignment, rather than the experience.

The structure that this commentary might take depends on the individual instructor, but generally emphasizes comparing this graded draft to previous drafts and future drafts, in order to underscore that the instructor is assessing the assignment. See Textbox 7.2 for an example of narrative formative commentary.

TEXTBOX 7.2. SAMPLE NARRATIVE FORMATIVE COMMENTARY

This submission shows a marked improvement over the rough draft you submitted last week. In that rough draft, the plot was often filled with digressions, and the dialogue did not seem to serve a purpose other than extending the length of the draft so that it met the minimum length requirement for the assignment. While the rough draft had a relevant experience at its core, that experience was sometimes lost in confusing plot points and extraneous dialogue. However, this latest draft demonstrates a significant improvement in those areas. The latest draft has eliminated the unnecessary dialogue and has tightened up the plot so that only the most important events are included. I would encourage you to keep revising this narrative for the portfolio. While this latest draft shows a significant improvement in the use of dialogue and the attention to the plot, the final draft in the portfolio should look to build on this already strong foundation by providing more advanced and experimental elements, like an *in media res* opener at the beginning of the narrative.

This example demonstrates some sample narrative formative commentary that Chris, for instance, might provide for a narrative. This commentary is formatted as a narrative by emphasizing its chronological order. To illustrate this chronological order, Chris deliberately compares the current draft to the previous draft of the narrative, and then he provides a destination for the narrative to aim for in the final draft of the essay in the writing portfolio.

Providing narrative formative commentary at the end of the comments for a narrative is more than just a clever intellectual exercise specifically designed for this book. This approach can help students to better understand that the instructor's commentary is directed at improving their work, rather than in critiquing their experiences. Chris demonstrates this in his sample comments in textbox 7.2, as he is careful to praise the experiences of the author while still providing constructive criticism to help revise the assignment.

CONCLUSION

Through much discussion and reassurance, Chris was finally able to explain to the student in the scene described at the beginning of this chapter that the object of his criticism was the narrative, rather than the student's experiences. This student (somewhat reluctantly, at first) came to understand that his own experience was a valued part of the narrative, and that Chris was only attempting to help to accentuate this experience through revision.

As this chapter demonstrates, Chris could have avoided this kind of confusion by incorporating a clear and comprehensive rubric and narrative formative commentary. An analytical rubric could help Chris to present the criteria for assessing the assignment in a form that is easy to read and understand.

The narrative formative commentary builds on the understanding of formative commentary as essentially concerned with formative instruction, or feedback that instructs students on how to complete an assignment or a task. In this case, the added step of utilizing a narrative structure—of providing a chronological order comparing the current assignment to previous submissions—can help students to see that the commentary is focused on the assignment rather than their experiences, and to hopefully use these comments during revision.

NOTE

1. Though many may prefer to use "summative" to describe the end comments to an essay—as the commentary is provided at the end of the student's attempts to demonstrate that she or he has acquired the skills needed to write in this particular genre—the phrase "formative" is used here to demonstrate the applicability of the suggestions offered in this chapter in classes that offer students the opportunity to revise.

REFERENCES

Arter, J., & McTighe, J. (2001). *Scoring rubrics in the classroom: Using performance criteria for assessing and improving student performance*. Thousand Oaks, CA: Corwin Press.
Goodrich, H. (1996). Understanding rubrics. *Educational Leadership, 54*(4), 14–17.
Liu, Y. (2013). Preliminary study on application of formative assessment in college English writing class. *Theory and Practice in Language Studies, 3*(12), 2186–2195.
Ussher, B., & Earl, K. (2010). "Summative" and "formative": Confused by the assessment terms? *New Zealand Journal of Teachers' Work, 7*(1), 53–63.

Chapter Eight

"Yes, But..."

Establishing a Language Base for Working with Stories

During the fall 2007 semester, Anthony's composition students finished their end-of-the-unit reflections on the essay that they were just about to submit. One by one, they shuffled the short, handwritten reflections into their folders and double-checked to make sure that their final drafts, first drafts, and peer reviews were all included and clearly labeled. Once ready, they made their way to the front of the dimly lit computer classroom and dropped their folders—some new and tidy, others torn and dirty—on the pile at the front desk, then returned to their seats.

Once all of the essays were submitted, Anthony swiftly distributed the prompt for the next essay, the fourth and final essay assignment of the semester. The students, just as they had when submitting the first two essay assignments, expressed surprise at the quick transition from the third to the fourth unit. One student even muttered, "No break in between?" with a pained expression on his face. The students' dismay grew heavier, as they all immediately flipped to the back of the page and saw the 6–8 pages length requirement.

The final research paper assignment, a synthesis essay, was part of the department's standardized composition course syllabus. The synthesis essay required students to bring together multiple argument-based sources on a similar topic, and forward an original thesis on a question about the texts. They were to select three texts from the classroom reader, an anthology of nonfiction texts grouped by topic, and then locate two remaining sources on the topic from the university library's online research databases.

Anthony and his students read through the prompt, discussing the requirements. "Any questions?" Anthony asked when they finished. Silence. Some students eventually said, "No." Some shrugged.

They spent the remainder of the period engaged in several activities that illustrated the concept of synthesis. In the waning moments of the session, at the start of the flutter of backpack zippers and scooting chairs, one student raised her hand. Flustered and trying to wrap her head around the assignment, she held up her copy of the class reader and asked, "So, you want us to read several stories in this book and then go to the library and find other stories that are similar and then talk about all of the stories together?"

Realizing that the question was loaded with more issues than he had time to address, Anthony offered a qualified "Yes" and dismissed the class.

In *Engaging Ideas*, Bean (2001) observed, "Many of today's students are poor readers, overwhelmed by the density of their college textbooks and baffled by the strangeness and complexity of primary sources and by their unfamiliarity with academic discourse" (p. 133). As part of this unfamiliarity, many students, like Anthony's, use "story" and "stories" as a generic genre term to identify any academic work, fiction or otherwise, that they read.

This overreliance on "story" as a blanket genre term stems, in part, from the specific practice of scholars, academic writers, and journalists to utilize stories, short anecdotes, and narrative elements within thesis-driven materials. As Bean (2001) argued, "Unlike experts, inexperienced readers are less apt to chunk complex material into discrete parts with describable functions" (p. 135). For example, when asked to summarize the thesis of an article that begins with a story or anecdote, some students may simply summarize that story, simply because it is up front.

Stories, as discussed in the previous chapters, have the power to break down barriers to learning. However, certain conditions and strategies must be in place for stories to be used effectively in a composition class. In other words, teachers must develop a language base for reading and analyzing stories, due to a common tendency of some first-year students who are new to academic discourse to label everything they read as a "story."

CONCEPTIONS OF GENRE

Diverse definitions of key terms and concepts, even seemingly straightforward terms like "story," can create tension, confusion, and frustration among students and teachers. While not much research focused on the specific issue of students using "story" or "stories" as a generic label, scholars have explored the broader issue of terminology in the classroom.

For example, in their investigation of potential themes or factors influencing the transfer of knowledge from composition, Nelms and Dively (2007) conducted a focus group with five professors in the College of Applied Sciences and Arts at a large research university. The participants held different conceptions of the term "persuasion," defining it as "justifying an opinion" or "explaining your reasoning" (p. 227). Based on this discussion, the researchers suspect that composition knowledge transfer is "constrained by significant vocabulary differences between general composition courses and discipline-specific courses" (p. 227).

Mullin, Reid, Enders, and Baldridge (1998) highlighted a similar instance of confusion over the use of the term "discuss" in a writing assignment requiring students to engage with source materials and course concepts. The authors documented efforts to embed a writing center tutor in a writing-intensive geography course. In working to fine-tune assignments in the course, the tutor observed that the term is often viewed within composition and writing studies as stating an opinion, while the instructors in geography use the term to engage source materials.

These studies suggested the need for explicit discussions of key terms, even those that appear to be self-explanatory. However, this notion of building a language base is not to restrict our understanding of stories, but to preserve their power and unique characteristics. Moreover, building a language base should not imply rigid definitions; stuffing academic discourse into static containers would not be productive, and would obscure the dynamic nature of most academic discourse.

Work with genre theory over the past few decades has moved past this static, container view, starting with Miller's landmark essay, "Genre as Social Action" (1984). She drew on rhetorical theory to analyze the link between genres and rhetorical situations. Moving beyond the view of genres as formal, pre-existing categories or containers, she asserted that genres are "typified rhetorical actions based in recurrent situations" (p. 159). In other words, genre is a social action, a response based on audience, context, and purpose. Writers construct and utilize specific genres to respond appropriately to a writing situation that they continually encounter.

As Devitt (2003) argued, this new conception of genre "shifts the focus from effects (formal features, text classifications) to sources of those effects" (pp. 270–271). Focusing on context, then, positions genre as a dynamic construct, changing and adapting to suit the needs of specific discourse communities as well as individuals. Genres, Devitt noted, "Change with society" (p. 276); as contexts change and new situations arise, genres adapt and new genres develop.

Russell argued (1997) that genres are only temporarily stabilized, as "context is an ongoing accomplishment" (p. 513). Building on Witte's analysis of genre, Russell later (1999) offered an example of how a text, specifically a list of food items, changes according to specific motives and objectives within different activity systems. The list, he explained, could serve as a family grocery list, "a tool for reducing temptation for a weight-loss group," an order form for supermarket buyers, and a grocery supplier's invoice (p. 82).

In this same way, texts that students will compose in FYC courses, such as a summary of a source text, will inevitably assume different shapes across the disciplines. A summary of an experiment for a biology lab needs to be thorough, employing clear and descriptive language to account for all the different variables and details. On the other hand, a summary of a film for a movie review needs to be concise, so as to not spoil plot details for potential viewers, but still must engage the reader and set up the review portion of the text. As these examples illustrate, connecting form to context reveals the shifting nature of genre.

In her review of research on genre, Clark (2003) argued that this new conception ultimately "provides a perspective that has potential for examining many different genres, real-world genres such as business letters or greeting cards as well as academic genres such as lab reports or school essays" (p. 243).

Indeed, Journet (1999) claimed that genre theory can provide insight into many questions about the writing processes of experienced and neophyte writers in the sciences. She has expounded on this theory by examining how scholars constructed and then developed the adaptive landscape metaphor, a genre convention in evolutionary biology, over time. This key example emphasizes the importance of viewing texts as processes and products "to understand the sociocognitive dimensions of writing" (p. 114).

Devitt assumed a broader view, arguing that genre theory could potentially "lead us to a unified theory of writing" by overcoming dichotomies that "threaten to undermine our holistic understanding of writing," specifically process and product, form and content, text and context, and the role of individuals within social situations (p. 270). Like Journet, Devitt (2003) positioned genre as both a process and product, but further advances the argument by illustrating how the new conception can unite text and context and link form to function, as well as highlight how individuals negotiate social processes. Despite these benefits, however, she observed that genre theory may not provide answers to many challenges and problems that composition teachers will encounter.

However, in the case of helping students perceive what they read, genre theory can be the answer, serving as a framework that allows us to preserve the dynamic nature of writing while still helping composition students to identify and describe the genres that they are reading and writing about. It is a way, as Swales (1990) argued, of "sensitizing students to rhetorical effects, and to the rhetorical structures that tend to recur in genre-specific texts" (p. 213).

STORYBOARDING

Armed with the notion that genres change and adapt based on context, teachers can craft lessons and activities that invite students to discuss and analyze how stories and narratives are utilized within other kinds of texts. Instead of assuming that students understand the genre of a particular text (and even understand the concept of "genre"), explicit discussions of genre can lead to a deeper understanding of the meaning of a text, as well as the rhetorical methods employed by the author.

When encountering texts that use stories and narrative elements—particularly those thesis-driven texts that begin with long, drawn-out narratives—a storyboard, or a storyboard outline, can be a useful tool. A storyboard, of course, is a genre used in film and other visual media to map out scenes in a story, set camera angles, and document scene changes. In terms of storytelling, storyboards can visualize scenes—particularly action sequences—and introduce pacing and movement. Filmmakers like Alfred Hitchcock, Ridley Scott, and George Lucas have used storyboards to translate abstract worlds from the script into concrete visuals. These qualities make storyboards useful tools for reading and analysis in the composition classroom.

With a focus on new literacies, composition scholars and practitioners are exploring the use of techniques and genres from film in writing instruction. Masserman (2015) explored how scene writing, as a creative prewriting tool, can help students "break down writing into basic and easily accessible parts" (p. 25). She adds that this method helps students see writing as more enjoyable, as well as demonstrate their comprehension of complex texts through multiple genres.

Storyboarding, specifically, can help students develop their critical thinking and reading comprehension skills. Recent scholarship highlighted the versatility of storyboarding as a creative prewriting tool. Lillyman, Gutteridge, and Berridge (2010) illustrated how nursing students can use storyboarding to reflect on their work with patients who are receiving end-of-life care. Love (2014), in contrast, developed a hip-hop-based education, using storyboarding to create narratives that capture the cultural identities of marginalized groups.

Bruce (2011) has demonstrated how storyboards can be framed as tools for active close reading. Appealing to visual learners, storyboarding allows students to translate texts into concrete, visual terms and focus on key images. In this way, storyboarding allows students to break down complex texts, developing their analytical and critical thinking skills. It shifts reading from passive to active, Bruce explained, "Creating storyboards encourages students to engage and interact—or in a reader-response term, *transact*—with the text" (p. 79). Bruce illustrated this approach with example exercises from fiction, poetry, and film.

Using a similar approach, storyboarding can help composition students analyze nonfiction texts. By visualizing an idea or image and writing a short description, students can begin to understand the various parts and how they work together. With texts that utilize narratives, specifically as a lead-in to an argumentative thesis, storyboarding can underscore how a story is used. The goal of this exercise is to reach some conclusion about which genre terms might best describe the text as a whole.

Storyboarding can be used as a writing activity at the beginning of a class period to jump-start discussion of a reading. A handout can be provided, or students can create their own storyboards on a blank sheet of paper. A basic storyboard includes a panel for a visual image and a short space for text. The visuals can be complex or simple stick figures; artistic skills are not necessary to complete this exercise effectively, as the main goal is to understand the reading from different perspectives. The following figures illustrate basic storyboard outlines.

Figure 8.1 is open, allowing students to map out the narrative elements of a text and make their own notes. The advantage of this approach is that it allows the students to visualize the text in more concrete terms, frame by frame, and produce notes that focus on their ideas and interpretations.

Figure 8.2 represents a more focused approach. Here, students must respond to specific questions about the narrative or story elements of a text. These questions direct students to understand how stories operate within a given text. It also asks students to reach some conclusions about how to classify the text, and determine if "story" is an accurate term to use in discussing the text overall. With this approach, students can visualize key elements of the story that relate to their responses to the questions.

With this second approach, instructors can develop the questions to produce a more directed discussion. Or, students can even write the questions first as a group, copy them down, and answer them. They can even provide visual representations of the text. In any configuration, this approach draws from genre theory; the goal is not to classify a text in a container, but to develop terms to refer to the text in discussions and in writing.

To illustrate these various approaches, let's consider an example of a thesis-driven text that begins with a detailed, image-laden narrative. In "Rural>City>Cyberspace: The Greatest Migration in Human History" (Carr, 2013), an article that is often anthologized, the author utilized research studies in psychology to argue that the Internet reduces our ability to concentrate and think critically. In turn, this erodes our compassion. The article begins

Name: _____
Date: ___/___/___

Storyboard Outline

[blank storyboard grid with 9 frames arranged 3×3]

Figure 8.1. Blank Storyboard Outline

with a narrative scene depicting a young Nathaniel Hawthorne, in order to introduce the idea that technology disrupts our concentration:

> It was a warm summer morning in Concord, Massachusetts. The year was 1844. An aspiring novelist named Nathaniel Hawthorne was sitting in a small clearing in the woods, a particularly peaceful spot known around town as Sleepy Hollow. Deep in concentration, he was attending to every passing impression, turning himself into what Emerson, the leader of Concord's Transcendentalist movement, had eight years earlier termed a "transparent eyeball." Hawthorne saw, as he would record in his notebook later that day, how "sunshine glimmers through shadow, and shadow effaces sunshine, imagining that pleasant mood of mind where gayety and pensiveness intermingle."

Name: _____
Date: ___/___/___

Storyboard Outline

[ ] -What is the role of a story or a narrative in this piece?	[ ] -Is there a central protagonist? Explain.	[ ] -Is there conflict in the story? Explain.
[ ] -Is there a central thesis in this piece? If yes, paraphrase the thesis in your own words.	[ ] -If yes, how does the story relate to the central thesis?	[ ] -Is the story or narrative sustained throughout the piece?
[ ] -Are there elements of other genres incorporated into this piece?	[ ] -What descriptive terms could you use to describe the genre of this piece?	[ ] -In your essay, what genre terms could you use when referring to this piece?

Figure 8.2. Storyboard Template with Sample Questions

He felt a slight breeze, "the gentlest sigh imaginable, yet with a spiritual potency, insomuch that it seems to penetrate, with its mild, ethereal coolness, through the outward clay, and breathe upon the spirit itself, which shivers with gentle delight." He smelled on the breeze a hint of "the fragrance of white pines." He heard "the striking of the village clock" and "at a distance mowers whetting their scythes," though "these sounds of labor, when at a proper remoteness, do but increase the quiet of one who lies at his ease, all in a mist of his own musings." (p. 95)

Carr continued, "Abruptly, his reverie is broken" (p. 95), as a locomotive whistle pierces the air. Quoting Hawthorne directly, Carr captured how this sound introduces the noise of the village, the clutter of technology that disrupts the peace and tranquility of the scene. From this narrative, Carr began to explore research studies on how urban and rural environments affect our focus and concentration.

The text, with its use of narrative and research studies, can be challenging for students, especially those who are new to argumentative texts. Storyboarding allows students to analyze, both visually and textually, the various components of Carr's work, and then brainstorm ways to talk about it.

As figure 8.3 illustrates, students can visualize key parts of the narrative, or even develop visuals that illustrate the responses themselves. The top three panels show how students can develop visual representations of key elements and then discuss those elements in their short answers below. The panels focus on the role of the story overall, down to specific elements, such as the use of a protagonist and a central conflict. This enables students to comprehend parts of the narratives from multiple perspectives, potentially increasing their understanding of the text.

Carr's introductory narrative, complete with lush, descriptive details pulled directly from Hawthorne's vivid account, immerses readers in the scene. There is a protagonist and conflict. Hawthorne, the young writer and thinker, is able to observe and reflect on the scene around him and the thoughts and emotions triggered by the tranquility of the environment. The locomotive, a force of technology, dominates the protagonist's sense of sight, smell, and sound. Thus, his productive bout of reflection is broken.

However, to consider Carr's article as a "story," overall, obscures key elements of his rhetorical situation. Drawing readers in and conveying the effects of a peaceful nature scene on an individual is a central component of his thesis. By painting this scene, via Hawthorne, Carr was better equipped to make his argument that "there is no sleepy hollow on the Internet" (p. 97). While the story is not sustained throughout the text, the basic conflict from the story informs the thesis and the research studies that are later incorporated as evidence.

The middle three panels of the storyboard expand the focus to the entire work. Specifically, students can explore if and how the reading utilizes a central thesis statement. The panels can then allow students to situate, in visual terms, the narrative elements of the story within the scope and aim of the thesis. In their written responses, students can paraphrase the thesis and explore how it is sustained throughout the text.

Finally, with the use of the last three panels, students can reach some working conclusions about the piece overall. As illustrated in figure 8.3, the questions should account for various perspectives and ask students to brainstorm multiple ways to identify and discuss the text. They should not simply classify a text in one fixed way, but develop several different terms to refer to a piece of writing. These questions can also point students toward looking at how authors synthesize and blend multiple genres.

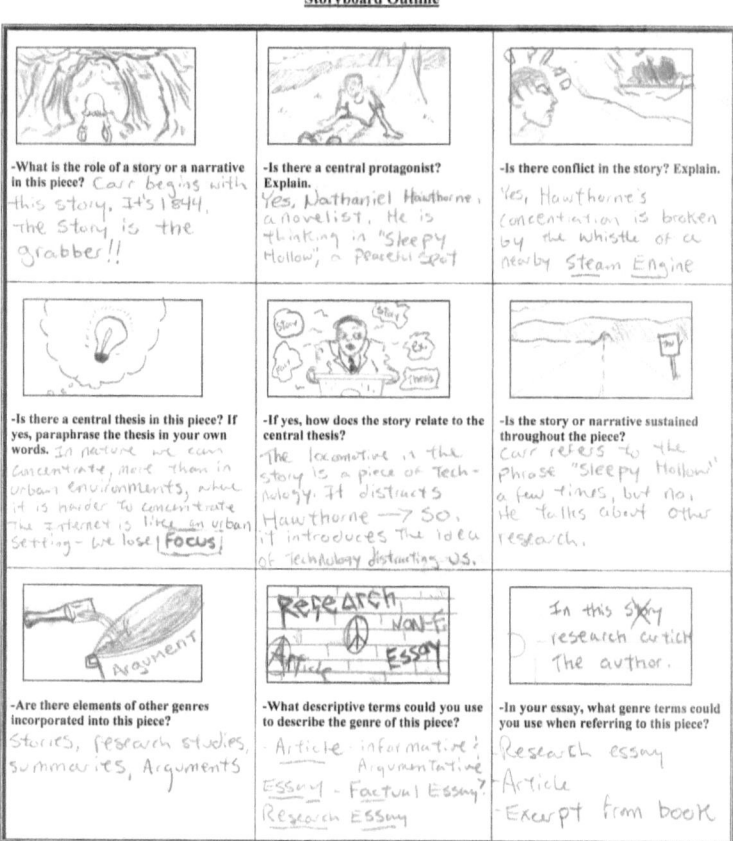

Figure 8.3. Completed Storyboard Outline

In his essay, Carr synthesized multiple research studies, stories, and other observations to forward his thesis about technology's influence on our thinking. In fact, the opening story is recreated through quotes and paraphrases; it can be viewed as a summary of a source text as much as a story or narrative. Brainstorming terms like "argument," "essay," "research study," "nonfiction article," and "synthesis" can help students to develop concrete terms that accurately describe the author's intent. Through storyboarding, students can take a complex and, at times, daunting article, and break it down into its essential parts.

As this discussion illustrates, storyboarding is a versatile activity; it can be used in a number of different ways, from a discussion starter to a homework assignment. Appealing to visual learners, storyboards provide alternate paths for thinking and writing about texts. At the same time, it can facilitate explicit discussions of genre and genre terms. Overall, then, this activity helps to build a language base for talking about stories and narratives.

CONCLUSION

Stories and narratives have the power to unlock students' potential and develop their writing and reading skills. However, in working to tap into that power, instructors must not make basic assumptions about students' understanding of stories and how they work. Students' definitions of what constitutes a story can be as varied as the experiences detailed in the stories and narratives that they read. While seemingly simple, terms like "story" and "narrative" are complex. Assuming that students understand these terms—particularly within genres that they may not be used to reading—and define them as we do, could result in confusion.

Thus, prior to diving into the immense and often overwhelming world of stories, instructors should engage in explicit discussions about basic terms. The central purpose of storyboarding and other activities and discussions is to build a vocabulary for discussing and writing about stories and narratives. Building a language base first can make for a more enriching experience in reading and writing stories in the writing classroom.

REFERENCES

Bean, J. C. (2001). *Engaging ideas*. San Francisco, CA: Jossey Bass.

Bruce, D. L. (2011). Framing the text: Using storyboards to engage students with reading. *English Journal, 100*(6), 78–85. Retrieved from http://www.ncte.org/journals/ej

Carr, N. (2013). Rural>city>cyberspace: The biggest migration in human history. In R. Bullock (Ed.), *The Norton Field Guide to Writing* (3rd ed.; pp. 95–100). New York, NY: Norton.

Clark, I. L. (Ed.). (2003). *Concepts in composition: Theory and practice in the teaching of writing*. Mahwah, NJ: Lawrence Erlbaum.

Devitt, A. J. (2003). Generalizing about genre: New conceptions of an old concept. In I. L. Clark (Ed.), *Concepts in composition* (pp. 270–283). Mahwah, NJ: Lawrence Erlbaum.

Journet, D. (1999). Writing within (and between) disciplinary genres: The "adaptive landscape" as a case study in interdisciplinary rhetoric. In T. Kent (Ed.), *Post-process theory: beyond the writing-process paradigm* (pp. 96–115). Carbondale, IL: Southern Illinois University Press.

Lillyman, S., Gutteridge, R., & Berridge, P. (2010). Using a storyboarding technique in the classroom to address end of life experiences in practice and engage student nurses in deeper reflection. *Nurse Education in Practice, 11*(3), 179–185. Retrieved from https://www.journals.elsevier.com/nurse-education-in-practice

Love, B. L. (2014). Urban storytelling: How storyboarding, moviemaking, and hip-hop-based education can promote students' critical voice. *English Journal, 103*(5), 53–58. Retrieved from http://www.ncte.org/journals/ej

Masserman, D. (2015). Lights, camera, write: How scene writing can help students write in multiple genres. *English Journal, 105*(2), 22–26.

Miller, C. R. (1984). Genre as social action. *Quarterly Journal of Speech, 70*, 151–167.

Mullin, J., Reid, N., Enders, D., & Baldridge, J. (1998). Constructing each other: Collaborating across disciplines and roles. In C. Peterson Haviland, M. Notarangelo, L. Whitley-Putz, & T. Wolf (Eds.), *Weaving knowledge together: Writing Centers and collaboration* (pp. 152–171). Emmitsburg, MD: NWCA.

Nelms, G., & Dively, R. L. (2007). Perceived roadblocks to transferring knowledge from first-year composition to writing-intensive major courses: A pilot study. *WPA: Writing Program Administration, 31*(1–2), 214–240.

Russell, D. R. (1997). Rethinking genre in school and society. *Written Communication, 14*(4), 504–554.

Russell, D. R. (1999). Activity theory and process approaches: Writing (power) in school and society. In T. Kent (Ed.), *Post-process theory: Beyond the writing process paradigm* (pp. 80–95). Carbondale and Edwardsville, IL: Southern Illinois University Press.

Swales, J. (1990). *Genre analysis: English in academic and research settings.* Cambridge, UK: Cambridge University Press.

Chapter Nine

Implications for New Teacher Training

The graduate students gathered, swiveling in their padded chairs around the U-shaped conference table as the instructor, clutching a familiar blue book, strolled in. On a steamy August day in 2004, Dr. Bryan Bardine, coordinator of graduate teaching assistants at the University of Dayton, convened the second day of a workshop for new composition instructors. He began the session the same way that he did the day before: with a story. Using *Comp Tales*, a collection of stories from composition teachers edited by R. H. Haswell and M. Lu (2000), Bardine offered a case to debate as a discussion starter.

A collection of oral stories of college composition, *Comp Tales* provided instructors with a guide for training new teachers, shaping teaching strategies and techniques, developing faculty and professional development forums, "getting the pulse of the profession," and reading for pleasure (p. xi). Each story, it should be noted, includes a short note from the contributor about how the story is often used in the classroom. The collection's editors also provide their own commentary on each tale at the end of each section.

On this particular day, Bardine shared a story from contributor M. M. Dossin (2000) about a student who became irate after earning a "D" on a paper about the death of his brother. During a meeting with Dossin, the student frantically shouted, "You gave a 'D' to my feelings," prompting Dossin to revisit the ways that she deals with "D" and "F" essays (p. 45). Like the story discussed in chapter 8, this scenario focused on how students often see grades on narratives as a reflection of the personal content.

After reading the story, Bardine asked the group of TAs to brainstorm how they would handle this situation. As second-year graduate students, Chris and Anthony offered their assessment of the case, along with their peers. The group discussed the use of grading rubrics, as well as strategies for conferencing with students. Many agreed that having a concrete grading rubric to refer to and discuss may have diffused some of the tension. Bardine then introduced the day's topic of responding to student work.

In this particular instance, the instructor, Bardine, was able to use a story to jump-start discussions and thread it to the work at hand in a productive way. Unlike the story that opened the introduction, this discussion did not digress into a series of other extreme stories, what some may refer to as a "group therapy session."

This final chapter, returning to a problem described in the introduction, will focus on using stories in workshops and training sessions for new teachers. Stories and narratives have immense power as training tools, but there is the danger that new teachers, particularly inexperienced TAs, can be overwhelmed by an onslaught of horror stories and worst-case scenarios. An abundance of teaching stories, or "comp tales," can stymie discussions, creating fear and tension. Thus, this chapter will offer a pragmatic tool for focusing class and workshop discussions that use teaching stories.

STORIES IN TEACHER TRAINING

The goal of most instructors when guiding whole-class discussion, as noted by McCann, Johannessen, Kahn, and Flanagan (2006), is to facilitate authentic discussions. Unlike recitation, which depends on clear-cut, "prespecified answers to the teacher's questions," authentic discussion invites skepticism, speculation, inquiry, and exploration (p. 3). To maintain discussions with the aim of airing ideas and exploring possibilities, as opposed to reaching a consensus, Wilhoit (2003) recommended that instructors synthesize comments and summarize key positions. Class discussions, Wilhoit urged, "should not end in confusion" (p. 119).

However, McCann et al. (2006) posited that offering an authentic question does not always foster authentic discussions. Questions can be met with silence, slow responses, and digressions. Compounding the problem is the fact that, while discussion is a tool for learning, it is not always the subject of learning. Barker (2015), drawing on distinctions by Parker and Hess (2001), reflected that she often "taught *with*, but not *for*, discussion," adding that she did not provide "explicit instruction on discussion skills" (p. 110). In both undergraduate and graduate courses, instructors like Barker must often engage in whole-class discussions without having the time or space to provide instruction on *how* to engage in such discussions.

In effect, fostering productive and authentic discussions can be a constant challenge, particularly in graduate or workshop settings with a cross-section of new and experienced teachers. In exploring dialogic exchanges, Wilhoit (2003) distinguished between open discussions, in which "students set the agenda," and more structured discussions that are set and moderated by an instructor (p. 118).

Scenario-based discussions can help to structure discussions and provides focus. McCann et al. (2006) argued that scenario activities, in which students discuss problematic situations, can facilitate useful discussions of abstract concepts, as well as provide insight into authentic discussions. The concept, according to the authors, stems from Aristotle's examination of courage in *Nicomachean Ethics*. An abstract concept, like courage, is defined and tested through various scenarios and situations. Participants then pose questions about those scenarios to peel back the layers of the subject at hand.

Teaching stories, or "comp tales," are a type of scenario activity. Stories and situations allow teachers to discuss key concepts, from revision to plagiarism, through sample narratives. By examining a story and then posing hypothetical questions (for example, "What if the instructor had asked the student to meet in her office, as opposed to discussing the issue in front of the class?"), participants can develop a deeper understanding of a concept. This also allows groups to brainstorm strategies for dealing with various kinds of problems and issues that may emerge during a semester.

Moreover, teaching stories can provide humor, comfort, and relief, allowing new teachers to see themselves as participants in a larger community of teachers. As Lu posited in *Comp Tales* (2000), these stories from members of the composition community provide distance and perspective that bring "incidents down to a level that we can deal with. If others have done it before, it cannot be so terrible. If others have endured, so can we" (p. 207).

Thus, when inviting new and experienced teachers to respond to a particular case or story with the goal of brainstorming teaching strategies, a more structured discussion may be ideal. Fostering a more structured discussion, however, involves not only developing specific questions, but also employing a rubric or heuristic to plan and maintain productive exchanges.

RUBRICS FOR TARGETED DISCUSSIONS

While narratives can help to facilitate authentic discussion, there is always a persistent danger of digressions. Stories, particularly the worst-case scenarios or the traditional "weird-things-which-have-happened-to-me," to use Lu's term (2000, p. 223), can turn a focused discussion into a competition of sorts, in which participants attempt to tell the most outrageous tale.

A discussion tool, such as a rubric or heuristic, can help to keep scenario discussions focused and productive. Chapter 7 provides a general overview of rubrics and how they could be used to assess narrative-based essays. Rubrics can be useful for explicating criteria for discussions, as well. Barker (2015) concluded that "not demystifying the moves that make for effective discussion" can disadvantage students, "especially those whose home language varieties did not neatly map onto the codes of academic discourse" (p. 110). In effect, tacit or unspoken rules for discussion that are often assumed can be explicated and clarified.

Despite a number of recent articles on evaluating (Wang, 2015) and developing (Solan & Linardopoulos, 2011; Wyss, Freedman, & Siebert, 2014), rubrics to assess online discussions, the literature has not provided many tools for guiding whole-class discussions in face-to-face contexts, particularly teacher training workshops. However, Barker's (2015) "analytic rubric for speaking and listening skills during whole-class discussion" (p. 110) in high school and college classrooms is a useful model. The rubric focused on three key domains: community, which involves active listening, speaking clearly, and responding thoroughly; argumentation, the quality and quantity of support used to back claims; and knowledge, which focuses on the application of discipline-specific terms and references to texts. There are four performance levels used to evaluate students' performance in each domain: exemplary, accomplished, developing, and emerging. This kind of tool can ultimately clarify criteria and expectations for discussions, holding students accountable while keeping discussions on track.

DESIGNING A RUBRIC FOR SCENARIO-BASED DISCUSSIONS

Applying this idea to the use of narratives in discussions during graduate courses and workshops, a rubric for teaching scenario-based discussions can achieve the same goals. An instructional rubric for scenario or story-based discussions (table 9.1) was developed with the goal of producing focused, productive discussions. This rubric is a tool for planning and moderating discussions that use a story or stories to jump-start debates on a specific topic or issue. Its goal is twofold: to keep whole-class discussions focused and thorough.

This rubric was designed primarily to be an instructional rubric, as opposed to a scoring rubric that is exclusively used for grading purposes. An instructional rubric (Andrade, 2005) helps to clarify expectations and focus instructions. The rubric for scenario-based discussions adheres to these tenets. It also draws on best practices from recent theories on outcomes-based assessment, utilizing clear language for performance-level descriptions. These performance-level descriptions are more holistic than numeric, using descriptive language to distinguish the various performance levels, as opposed to using error counting.

Table 9.1. Rubric for Scenario-based Discussions

	Excellent	Good	Developing	Underdeveloped
Questioning	Points:	Points:	Points:	Points:
	The story is carefully framed within the context of a question to invite detailed responses on the topic/issue. The question is concrete and specific: it is evaluative, inviting participants to evaluate the situation or the teacher's performance within the situation, or hypothetical, offering participants "what if" variations of the scenario to consider and analyze. Clearly articulated and thought-provoking, the question propels the discussion forward toward new insights and avenues of debate on the topic/issue at hand.	The story is clearly framed within the context of a question that invites responses on the topic/issue. The question is specific, but one or two details need to be clarified. Though there are one or two unclear wording issues, the question is evaluative or hypothetical, advancing the discussion toward new insights related to the topic/issue at hand.	The story is framed with a question, but the question could be more specific. The question is evaluative, but is more general (i.e., "what do you think?") The question may prompt some productive responses, but also leads to one or two digressions or unrelated stories.	The story offered is engaging but is not connected to a specific question. It may prompt short, surface-level responses or other stories, but does not progress the discussion of the topic/issue at hand.
Relevance	Points:	Points:	Points:	Points:
	The story offered directly aligns with the topic/issue at hand. The story contains a conflict that reveals the nuances of the topic/issue that can be discussed and analyzed. Stories offered by participants in response adhere	The story offered clearly aligns with the topic/issue at hand, though, one or two details may need to be clarified. The story's conflict illustrates the topic/issue and can be analyzed and discussed. Stories offered by	The story offered tangentially relates to the topic/issue at hand, but it does contain a central conflict that can be discussed. Stories	The story offered does not relate to topic/issue at hand. It is more of an anecdote about an odd event more than a conflict that can be analyzed and discussed. Stories offered by participants in response do

	Excellent	Good	Developing	Underdeveloped
	to the criteria above, avoiding digressions from the subject.	participants in response match the criteria above, avoiding significant digressions from the subject.	offered by participants tangentially relate to and digress from the topic.	not relate to topic/issue, digressing from the task at hand.
	Points:	Points:	Points:	Points:
Specificity	The story offered is creatively and carefully told, using concrete descriptions and details to paint a vivid picture of the situation and those involved. In addition, the story features multiple strategies for dealing with the conflict that can be analyzed.	The story offered is engaging, using specific descriptions and details to depict the situation and people involved, though one or two minor points could be clarified. The story offers one or two concrete strategies for dealing with the conflict that can be analyzed.	The story offered has an engaging premise, but several key details regarding the situation and people need to be clarified and illustrated further. Though lacking in specific detail, the story does offer at least one strategy that could be analyzed.	The story offered is a general anecdote, lacking in key details regarding the situation and people. The story does not feature any strategies for dealing with the conflict. For instance, it may detail an odd or inappropriate student comment, but does not include how the instructor dealt with the comment.

The rubric also obeys the law of distal diminishment (Turley & Gallagher, 2008), which stipulated that a rubric, or any educational tool, "becomes less instructionally useful—and more potentially damaging to educational integrity—the farther away from the classroom it originates or travels" (p. 88). Designed to respond to a specific problem, the rubric focuses on criteria that directly link to that original situation. Thus, it does not include criteria that may be found in a rubric for evaluating discussions in general, such as listening skills, tone, or comprehension.

Three basic domains used to evaluate the use of teaching-based stories: questioning, relevance, and specificity ("QRS"). First, "questioning" refers to the quality and nature of the questions that are paired with the story. This domain measures whether the story is told within the context of a question, and whether that question can propel the discussion in meaningful ways.

"Relevance" focuses on connectivity, and how directly the story relates to the topic or issue at the center of a lesson plan. It also assesses whether the story contains a central conflict that can be evaluated or discussed. If no conflict is present, the story may just be an anecdote with the goal of entertaining or shocking audiences.

Finally, "specificity" looks at how the story is told, focusing on the level of details provided about the situation and those involved. In particular, this domain also evaluates whether specific strategies for dealing with the situation are featured in the telling of the story. For instance, if a story only relays an odd occurrence without detailing how the teacher dealt with that situation, it may invite responses but not offer potential strategies for new teachers, nor prompt a prolonged exchange.

APPLYING A RUBRIC FOR SCENARIO-BASED DISCUSSIONS

Instructors and workshop moderators can use this rubric in a number of ways. First, it can be used as a tool for planning. When preparing for a whole-class discussion, an instructor can use this rubric to select an appropriate story, either from his or her own experiences or from a published collection, that connects to the topic or issue to be debated. The rubric can then be applied in developing and shaping discussion questions. A particular story does not have to fall into the "excellent" performance level to prompt directed and detailed discussions. A story may be a simple anecdote lacking in detail, but could be paired with a nuanced question, for example.

Second, after the planning stage, an instructor can also use the rubric as tool for moderating the discussion. The rubric could be applied in posing a story and questions and keep the discussion focused. As the discussion unfolds, the instructor can use the rubric while listening to participants respond to questions and offer other stories. Used in this way, the rubric could help instructors ask participants to clarify or reframe their responses.

Of course, instructors can share this rubric, or a variation of it, with participants, explicating their expectations for scenario-based discussions. The "relevance" domain, in particular, could be used to evaluate subsequent stories offered by participants in their responses. While the rubric may be too narrowly devised to grade students or participants for all whole-class discussions, it could help to keep story-based evaluations focused and productive.

CONCLUSION

The development of a rubric to guide whole-class discussions here should not imply that trading horror stories has no value. Certainly, there is a time and a place to collect those worst-case scenarios. These kinds of sessions can certainly build camaraderie among new teachers. Telling these kinds of stories can also be cathartic. However, in situations where specific concepts and strategies must be analyzed and discussed, more focused discussions of stories can prove useful.

Ultimately, the tools developed in the chapters of this second part of the book on implications are not intended to limit the possibilities of stories. Instead, they help to provide focus, clarity, and understanding. Oftentimes, it can be cathartic to pile stories on top of each other around the dinner table; however, there are times when focus and clarity can enhance the use of a well-told story or narrative. Thus, when someone asks, "Tell me a story," or states, "Let me tell you a story," it can be savored, connected, and understood on a deeper level.

REFERENCES

Andrade, H. G. (2005). Teaching with rubrics: The good, the bad, and the ugly. *College Teaching, 53*(1), 27–30.

Barker, L. M. (2015). Under discussion: Teaching speaking and listening. *English Journal, 104* (5), 110–113.

Dossin, M. M. (2000). 37. In R. H. Haswell & M. Lu (Eds.), *Comp Tales* (pp. 45–46). New York, NY: Longman.

Haswell, R. & Lu, M. (Eds.). (2000). *Comp tales*. New York, NY: Longman.

Lu, M. (2000). Tracking comp tales. In R. H. Haswell and M. Lu (Eds.), *Comp tales*. New York, NY: Longman.

McCann, T. M., Johannessen, L. R., Kahn, E., & Flanagan, J. M. (2006). *Talking in class: Using discussion to enhance teaching and learning*. Urbana, IL: NCTE.

Parker, W. C., and Hess, D. (2001). Teaching with and for discussion. *Teaching and Teacher Education, 17*(3), 273–289.

Solan, A. M., & Linardopoulos, N. (2001). Development, implementation, and evaluation of a grading rubric for online discussions. *Journal of Online Learning and Teaching, 7*(4), 452–464.

Turley, E. D., & Gallagher, C. W. (2008). On the uses of rubrics: Reframing the great rubric debate. *English Journal, 97*(4), 87–92.

Wang, P. A. (2015). Assessment of asynchronous online discussions for a constructive online learning community. *International Journal of Information and Education Technology, 5*(8), 598–604.

Wilhoit, S. W. (2003). *The Allyn and Bacon teaching assistant's handbook: A guide for graduate instructors of writing and literature.* New York, NY: Longman.

Wyss, V. L., Freedman, D., & Siebert, C. J. (2014). The development of a discussion rubric for online courses: Standardizing expectations of graduate students in online scholarly discussions. *TechTrends, 58* (2), 99–107.

Bibliography

Abrami, P. C., Bernard, R. M., Bures, E. M., Borokhovski, E., & Tamin, R. (2011). Interaction in distance education and online learning: Using evidence and theory to improve practice. *Journal of Computing in Higher Education 23*, 82–103. doi:10.1007/s12528-011-9043-x
Adams, J., & Adams, A. S. (2004). *The letters of John and Abigail Adams.* F. Shuffelton (Ed.). New York, NY: Penguin.
Alexander, J. C. (2004). Toward a theory of cultural trauma. In J. C. Alexander, R. Eyerman, B. Giesen, N. Smelser, & P. Sztompka (Eds.), *Cultural trauma and collective identity* (pp. 1–30). Berkeley, CA: University of California Press.
Alexander, K. P. (2015). From story to analysis: Reflection and uptake in the literacy narrative assignment. *Composition Studies, 43*(2), 43–71.
Ambrose, S. E. (2002). Introduction. In D. K. Webster (Ed.), *Parachute infantry: An American paratrooper's memoir of D-Day and the fall of the Third Reich* (pp. ix–xvi). New York, NY: Delta.
Andrade, H. G. (2005). Teaching with rubrics: The good, the bad, and the ugly. *College Teaching, 53*(1), 27–30.
Appling-Jenson, B., Anzai, C., & Gonzalez, K. (2014). Bringing passion to the research process: The I-Search paper. In M. L. Warner (Ed.), *Teaching writing grades 7–12 in an era of assessment: Passion and practice* (pp. 130–152). Boston: Pearson.
Arter, J., & McTighe, J. (2001). *Scoring rubrics in the classroom: Using performance criteria for assessing and improving student performance.* Thousand Oaks, CA: Corwin Press.
Assaf, L. C., Ash, G. E., Saunders, J., & Johnson, J. (2011). Renewing two seminal literacy practices: I-Charts and I-Search papers. *Voices from the Middle, 18*(4), 31–42.
Barker, L. M. (2015). Under discussion: Teaching speaking and listening. *English Journal, 104* (5), 110–113.
Bar-On, T. (2007). A meeting with clay: Individual narratives, self-reflection, and action. *Psychology of Aesthetics, Creativity, and the Arts, 1*(4), 225–236.
Bean, J. C. (2001). *Engaging ideas.* San Francisco, CA: Jossey-Bass.
Bergman, L. S. (2009). *Academic research and writing: Inquiry and argument in college.* Boston: Longman.
Binks, E., Smith, D. L., Smith, L. J., & Joshi, R. M. (2009). Tell me your story: Reflection strategy for preservice teachers. *Teacher Education Quarterly, 36*(4), 141–156.
Bishop, W. (2000). *The subject is reading.* Portsmouth, NH: Boynton/Cook.
Boud, D. (2001). Using journal writing to enhance reflective practice. In L. M. English & M. A. Gillen (Eds.), *Promoting journal writing in adult education: New directions for adult and continuing education* (pp. 9–18). San Francisco, CA: Jossey-Bass.

Boyle, E., & Rothstein, H. (2003). The first class sessions: Engaging students immediately. Chapter 12 in *Essentials of college and university teaching: A practical guide* (61–67). Stillwater, OK: New Forums Press.

Bradbury-Jones, C., Hughes, S. M., Murphy, W., Parry, L., & Sutton, J. (2009). A new way of reflecting in nursing: The Peshkin approach. *Journal of Advanced Nursing, 65*(11), 2485–2493.

Brady, D. W., Corbie-Smith, G., & Branch, W. T., Jr. (2002). "What's important to you?": The use of narratives to promote self-reflection and to understand the experiences of medical residents. *Annals of Internal Medicine, 137*(3), 220–223.

Branch, M., Min, D., & Anderson, M. (1999). Storytelling as a teaching-learning tool with RN students. *ABNF Journal, 10*(6), 131–135.

Brereton, J. C. (Ed.). (1995). *The origins of composition studies in the American college, 1875–1925: A documentary history*. Pittsburgh, PA: University of Pittsburgh Press.

Bruce, D. L. (2011). Framing the text: Using storyboards to engage students with reading. *English Journal, 100*(6), 78–85. Retrieved from http://www.ncte.org/journals/ej

Bryson, K. (2012). The literacy myth in the digital archive of literacy narratives. *Computers and Composition, 29*, 254–268. http://dx.doi.org/10.1016/j.compcom.2012.06.001

Bullock, R. (2013). *The Norton field guide to writing* (3rd ed.). New York, NY: Norton.

Burns, H. W., & MacBride, M. (2016). *Intellectual creativity in first-year composition classes*. Lanham, MD: Rowman & Littlefield.

Carr, N. (2013). Rural>city>cyberspace: The biggest migration in human history. In R. Bullock (Ed.), *The Norton Field Guide to Writing* (3rd ed.; pp. 95–100). New York, NY: Norton.

Charney, D., Newman, J. H., & Palmquist, M. (1995). "I'm just no good at writing": Epistemological style and attitudes toward writing. *Written Communication, 12*(3), 298–329.

Chi, F. M. (2010). Reflection as teaching inquiry: Examples from Taiwanese in-service teachers. *Reflective Practice, 11*(2), 171–183.

Chlup, D. T., & Collins, T. E. (2010). Breaking the ice: Using ice-breakers and re-energizers with adult learners. *Adult Learning, 21*, 34–39.

Clark, I. L. (Ed.). (2003). *Concepts in composition: Theory and practice in the teaching of writing*. Mahwah, NJ: Lawrence Erlbaum.

Cochran, J. D., Campbell, S. M., Baker, H. M., & Leads, E. M. (2014). The role of student characteristics in predicting retention in online courses. *Research in Higher Education, 55*, 27–48. doi:10.1007s11162-013-9305-8

Coker, F. H., & Scarboro, F. (1990). Writing to learn in upper-division sociology courses: Two case studies. *Teaching Sociology, 18*(2), 218–222.

Conference on College Composition and Communication. (2013, March). *A position statement of principles and example effective practices for online writing instruction*. Retrieved from http://www.ncte.org/cccc/resources/positions/owiprinciples

Conference on College Composition and Communication. (2014). *Writing assessment: A position statement*. Retrieved from http://www.ncte.org/cccc/resources/positions/writingassessment

Connors, R. J. (1997). *Composition-rhetoric: Backgrounds, theory, and pedagogy*. Pittsburgh, PA: University of Pittsburgh Press.

Conway, G. (1994). Portfolio cover letters, students' self-presentation, and teachers' ethics. In L. Black, D. A. Daiker, J. Sommers, & G. Stygall (Eds.), *New directions in portfolio assessment* (pp. 83–92). Portsmouth, NH: Boynton/Cook.

Cooley, T. (2012). *Back to the lake*. (2nd ed.). New York, NY: Norton.

Corkery, C. (2005). Literacy narratives and confidence building in the writing classroom. *Journal of Basic Writing, 24*(1), 48–67.

Daniell, B. (1999). Narrative of literacy: Connecting composition to culture. *College Composition and Communication, 50*(3), 393–410.

Davidson, M. R. (2004). A phenomenological evaluation: Using storytelling as a primary teaching method. *Nurse Education in Practice, 4*(3), 184–189. http://dx.doi.org.ezproxy.pgcc.edu/10.1016/S1471-5953(03)00043-X

Deaver, S. P., & McAuliffe, G. (2009). Reflective visual journaling during art therapy and counseling internships: A qualitative study. *Reflective Practice, 10*(5), 615–632.

Devitt, A. J. (2003). Generalizing about genre: New conceptions of an old concept. In I. L. Clark (Ed.), *Concepts in composition* (pp. 270–283). Mahwah, NJ: Lawrence Erlbaum.

Dohrer, G. (1991). Do teachers' comments on students' papers help? *College Teaching, 39*(2), 48–54.

Dorn, D. S. (1987). The first day of class: Problems and strategies. *Teaching Sociology, 15*(1), 61–72.

Dossin, M. M. (2000). 37. In R. H. Haswell & M. Lu (Eds.), *Comp Tales* (pp. 45–46). New York, NY: Longman.

Douglass, F. (1987). Narrative of the life of Frederick Douglass. In H. L. Gates (Ed.), *The Classic Slave Narratives* (pp. 243–331). New York, NY: Mentor.

Downs, D., & Wardle, E. (2007). Teaching about writing, righting misconceptions: (Re)envisioning "first-year composition" as "introduction to writing studies." *College Composition and Communication, 58*(4), 552–585.

Drouin, M. A. (2008). The relationship between students' perceived sense of community and satisfaction, achievement, and retention in an online course. *Quarterly Review of Distance Education, 9*(3), 267–284.

Duberstein, A. (2009). Building student-faculty relationships. *Academic Advising Today, 32*(1). Retrieved from http://www.nacada.ksu.edu/Resources/Academic-Advising-Today/View-Articles/Building-Student-Faculty-Relationships.aspx

Edwards, R. M., Cleland, J., Bailey, K., McLachlan, S., & McVey, L. (2009). Pharmacist prescribers' written reflection on developing their consultation skills. *Reflective Practice, 10*(4), 437–450.

Elbow, P. (1994). Will the virtues of portfolios blind us to their potential dangers? In L. Black, D. A. Daiker, J. Sommers, & G. Stygall (Eds.), *New directions in portfolio assessment,* (pp. 40–55). Portsmouth, NH: Boynton/Cook.

Elbow, P., & Belanoff, P. (1986). Portfolios as a substitute for proficiency examinations. *College Composition and Communication 37*(3), 336–339.

Eldred, J. C., & Mortensen, P. (1992). Reading literacy narratives. *College English, 54*(5), 512–539.

English, L. M. (2001). Ethical concerns relating to journal writing. In L. M. English & M. A. Gillen (Eds.), *Promoting journal writing in adult education*: *New directions for adult and continuing education* (pp. 27–35). San Francisco, CA: Jossey-Bass.

Eubanks, P., & Schaeffer, J. D. (2008). A kind of word for bullshit: The problem with academic writing. *College Composition and Communication, 59*(3), 372–388.

Feldbusch, R. (2007). Seeing academic writing with a new "I." *National Writing Project.* January. Retrieved from http://www.nwp.org/cs/public/print/resource/2371

Fracareta, P., & Phillips, D. J. (2000). Working with a writer's notebook. *English Journal, 89*(6), 105–113.

Frank, A. (1967). *Diary of a young girl*. New York, NY: Doubleday.

Furrer, C. J., Skinner, E. A., & Pitzer, J. R. (2014). The influence of teacher and peer relationships on students' classroom engagement and everyday motivational resilience. *National Society for the Study of Education, 113*(1), 101–123.

Gaffney, J. D. H., & Whitaker, J. T. (2015). Making the most of your first day of class. *The Physics Teacher, 53*, 137–139. http://dx.doi.org/10.1119/1.4908079

Glazier, R. A. (2016). Building rapport to improve retention and success in online classes. *Journal of Political Science Education, 12*(4), 1–20. doi:10.1080/15512169.2016.1155994

Goggin, P. N., & Goggin, M. D. (2006). Presence in absence: Discourses and teaching (in, on, and about) trauma. In Shane Borrowman (Ed.), *Trauma and the teaching of writing* (pp. 29–52). Albany, NY: State University of New York Press.

Goldblatt, E. (2017). Don't call it expressivism: Legacies of a "tacit tradition." *College Composition and Communication, 68*(3), 438–465.

Goldstein, G. S., & Benassi, V. A. (1994, December). The relation between teacher self-disclosure and student classroom participation. *Teaching of Psychology, 21*(4), 212–217.

Goodrich, H. (1996). Understanding rubrics. *Educational Leadership, 54*(4), 14–17.

Grace, C. M., Smith, K., & Hinchman, K. (2004). Exploring the African American oral tradition: Instructional implications for literacy learning. *Language Arts, 81*(6), 481–490.

Graff, H. J. (1979). *The literacy myth: Cultural integration and social structure in the nineteenth century.* New Brunswick, NJ: Transaction.

Hagemann, J. A. (2003). Helping students acquire the language of the academy. In C. R. Boiarsky (Ed.), *Academic literacy in the English classroom* (pp. 131–144). Portsmouth, NH: Boynton/Cook.

Harbin, J., & Humphrey, P. (2010). Teaching management by telling stories. *Academy of Educational Leadership Journal, 14*(1), 99–106.

Haswell, R. & Lu, M. (Eds.). (2000). *Comp tales.* New York, NY: Longman

Henze, B., Selzer, J., & Sharer, W. (2007). *1977: A cultural moment in composition.* West Lafayette, IN: Parlor Press.

Heo, M. (2009). Digital storytelling: An empirical study of the impact of digital storytelling on pre-service teachers' self-efficacy and dispositions towards educational technology. *Journal of Educational Multimedia and Hypermedia, 18*(4), 405–428.

Hillocks, G., Jr. (2007). *Narrative writing: Learning a new model for teaching.* Portsmouth, NH: Heinemann.

Hunt, D. (2002). *Misunderstanding the assignment: Teenage students, college writing, and the pains of growth.* Portsmouth, NH: Boynton Cook.

Joinson, A. N. (2001). Self-disclosure in computer mediated communication: The role of self-awareness and visual anonymity. *European Journal of Social Psychology 31*(2): 177–192. doi:10.1002/ejsp.36

Journet, D. (1999). Writing within (and between) disciplinary genres: The "adaptive landscape" as a case study in interdisciplinary rhetoric. In T. Kent (Ed.), *Post-process theory: beyond the writing-process paradigm* (pp. 96–115). Carbondale and Edwardsville, IL: Southern Illinois University Press.

Karkabi, K., Wald, H. S., & Castel, O. C. (2014). The use of abstract paintings and narratives to foster reflective capacity in medical educators: A multinational faculty development workshop. *Med Humanit, 40,* 44–48. doi:10.1136/medhum-2013-010378

Karnezis, G. T. (1998). Reclaiming "creativity" for composition. In D. Starkey (Ed.), *Teaching writing creatively* (pp. 29–42). Portsmouth, NH: Boynton/Cook.

King, R. S. (2013). They ask, should we tell? Thoughts on disclosure in the classroom. *The NEA Higher Education Journal, 29*(Fall), 101–111.

Koening, J. M., & Zorn, C. (2002). Using storytelling as an approach to teaching and learning with diverse students. *Journal of Nursing Education, 41*(9), 393–399.

Ku, H.-Y., Tseng, H. W., & Akarasriworn, C. (2013). Collaboration factors, teamwork satisfaction, and student attitudes toward online collaborative learning. *Computers in Human Behavior, 29*(3), 922–929. doi:10.1016/j.chb.2012.12.019

LaCapra, D. (2001). *Writing history, writing trauma.* Baltimore, MD: Johns Hopkins University Press.

LaCapra, D. (2004). *History in transit: Experience, identity, critical theory.* Ithaca, NY: Cornell University Press.

LaCapra, D. (2009). *History and its limits: Human, animal, violence.* Ithaca, NY: Cornell University Press.

Langley, M., & Brown, S. (2010). Perceptions of the use of reflective learning journals in online graduate nursing education. *Nursing Education Perspectives, 31*(1), 12–17.

Laub, D. (1995). Truth and testimony: The process and the struggle. In Cathy Caruth (Ed.), *Trauma: Explorations in memory* (pp. 61–75). Baltimore, MD: Johns Hopkins University Press.

Levett-Jones, T. L. (2007). Facilitating reflective practice and self-assessment of competence through the use of narratives. *Nurse Education in Practice, 7,* 112–119.

Lillyman, S., Gutteridge, R., & Berridge, P. (2010). Using a storyboarding technique in the classroom to address end of life experiences in practice and engage student nurses in deeper reflection. *Nurse Education in Practice, 11*(3), 179–185. Retrieved from https://www.journals.elsevier.com/nurse-education-in-practice

Liu, Y. (2013). Preliminary study on application of formative assessment in college English writing class. *Theory and Practice in Language Studies, 3*(12), 2186–2195.

Love, B. L. (2014). Urban storytelling: How storyboarding, moviemaking, and hip-hop-based education can promote students' critical voice. *English Journal, 103*(5), 53–58. Retrieved from http://www.ncte.org/journals/ej

Lu, M. (2000). Tracking comp tales. In R. H. Haswell and M. Lu (Eds.), *Comp tales*. New York, NY: Longman.

Luther, J. (2006). I-Searching in context: Thinking critically about the research unit. *English Journal, 95*(4), 68–74. doi:10.2307/30047092

MacGregor, J. (1993). Learning self-evaluation: Challenges for students. In J. MacGregor (Ed.), *Student Self-Evaluation: Fostering Reflective Learning* (pp. 35–46). San Francisco, CA: Jossey-Bass.

Macrorie, K. (1979). Textbooks that don't embalm. *New York Times*, September 3, p. A15.

Macrorie, K. (1984, 1988). *The I-Search paper* (Revised edition of *Searching writing*). Portsmouth, NH: Boynton/Cook.

Masserman, D. (2015). Lights, camera, write: How scene writing can help students write in multiple genres. *English Journal, 105*(2), 22–26.

Mazer, J. P., Murphy, R. E., & Simonds, C. J. (2007). I'll see you on "Facebook": The effects of computer-mediated teacher self-disclosure on student motivation, affective learning, and classroom climate. *Communication Education, 56*(1), 1–17.

McAteer, M., & Dewhurst, J. (2010). Just thinking about stuff: Reflective learning: Jane's story. *Reflective Practice, 11*(1), 33–43.

McCann, T. M., Johannessen, L. R., Kahn, E., & Flanagan, J. M. (2006). *Talking in class: Using discussion to enhance teaching and learning*. Urbana, IL: NCTE.

McCarthy, L. P. (1994). A stranger in strange lands: A college student writing across the curriculum. In C. Bazerman & D. Russell (Eds.), *Landmark essays on writing across the curriculum* (pp. 125–154). Mahwah, NJ: Erlbaum, 1994.

McCourt, F. (2005). *Teacher man*. New York, NY: Scribner.

McGinley, J. J., & Jones, B. D. (2014). A brief instructional intervention to increase students' motivation on the first day of class. *Teaching of Psychology, 41*(2), 158–162.

McKenzie, B., & Fitzsimmons, P. (2010). Optimising personal and professional reflection in a unique environment: Making sense of an overseas professional experience. *Reflective Practice, 11*(1), 45–56.

Micari, M., & Pazos, P. (2012). Connecting to the professor: Impact of the student-faculty relationship in a highly challenging course. *College Teaching, 60*(2), 41–47.

Miller, A. N., Katt, J. A., Brown, T., & Sivo, S. A. (2014). The relationship of instructor self-disclosure, nonverbal immediacy, and credibility to student incivility in the college classroom. *Communication Education, 63*(1), 1–16.

Miller, C. R. (1984). Genre as social action. *Quarterly Journal of Speech, 70*, 151–167.

Mullin, J., Reid, N., Enders, D., & Baldridge, J. (1998). Constructing each other: Collaborating across disciplines and roles. In C. Peterson, M. Haviland, M. Notarangelo, L. Whitley-Putz, & T. Wolf (Eds.), *Weaving knowledge together: Writing centers and collaboration* (pp. 152–171). Emmitsburg, MD: NWCA.

Murray, D. (1982). Teaching the other self: The writer's first reader. *College Composition and Communication, 33*(2), 140–147.

Neal, M. (1998). The politics and perils of portfolio grading. In F. Zak & C. C. Weaver (Eds.), *The theory and practice of grading writing: Problems and possibilities* (pp. 123–138). Albany, NY: State University of New York Press.

Nelms, G., & Dively, R. L. (2007). Perceived roadblocks to transferring knowledge from first-year composition to writing-intensive major courses: A pilot study. *WPA: Writing Program Administration, 31*(1–2), 214–240.

North, S. (1987). *The making of knowledge in composition: Portrait of an emerging field*. Upper Montclair, NJ: Boynton.

North, S. (1987). Writing in a philosophy class: Three case studies. In T. Fulwiler (Ed.), *The journal book* (pp. 278–288). Portsmouth, NH: Boynton/Cook.

O'Brien, T. (1990). *The things they carried*. New York, NY: Broadway.

Ollerenshaw, J. A., & Lowery, R. (2006). Storytelling: Eight steps that help you engage your students. *Voices from the Middle, 14*(1), 30–37.

Parker, W. C., & Hess, D. (2001). Teaching with and for discussion. *Teaching and Teacher Education, 17*(3), 273–289.

Parkinson, D. D. (2005). Unexpected student reflections from an underused genre. *College Teaching, 53*(4), 147–151.

Ramsey, C. A. (2000). Storytelling can be a valuable teaching aid. *Association of Operating Room Nurses, 72*(3), 497–499.

Rester, C. H., & Edwards, R. (2007). Effects of sex and setting on students' interpretation of teachers' excessive use of immediacy. *Communication Education, 56*(1), 34–53.

Robinson, T. A., & Burton, V. T. (2012). The writer's personal profile: Student self-assessment and goal setting at start of term. In T. M. Zawacki & P. M. Rogers (Eds.), *Writing across the curriculum: A critical sourcebook* (pp. 508–523). Boston: Bedford/St. Martin's.

Russ, T. L., Simonds, C. J., & Hunt, S. K. (2002). Coming out in the classroom . . . an occupational hazard?: The influence of sexual orientation on teaching credibility and perceived student learning. *Communication Education, 51*(3), 311–324.

Russell, D. R. (1997). Rethinking genre in school and society. *Written Communication, 14*(4), 504–554.

Russell, D. R. (1999). Activity theory and process approaches: Writing (power) in school and society. In T. Kent (Ed.), *Post-process theory: Beyond the writing process paradigm* (pp. 80–95). Carbondale and Edwardsville, IL: Southern Illinois University Press.

Ryden, W. (2005). Conflicted literacy: Frederick Douglass' critical model. *Journal of Basic Writing, 24*(1), 4–23.

Sanders, L., Daly, A. P., & Fitzgerald, K. (2016). Predicting retention, understanding attrition: A prospective study of foundation year students. *Widening Participation and Lifelong Learning, 16*(2), 50–75. doi:10.5456/WPLL.18.2.50

Sassoon, S. (1930). *Memoirs of an infantry officer.* New York, NY: Coward-McCann.

Schuster, C. I. (1994). Climbing the slippery slope of assessment: The programmatic use of writing portfolios. In L. Black, D. A. Daiker, J. Sommers, & G. Stygall (Eds.), *New directions in portfolio assessment,* (pp. 314–324). Portsmouth, NH: Boynton/Cook.

Shadiow, L. K. (2009). The first day of class: How it matters. *The Clearing House, 82*(4), 197–200.

Short, K. G. (2014). *NCTE 104th annual convention program.* Washington, DC: NCTE.

Simon, L. (1991). De-coding writing assignments. *The History Teacher, 24*(2), 149–155. Retrieved from http://www.jstor.org/stable/49412

Solan, A. M., & Linardopoulos, N. (2001). Development, implementation, and evaluation of a grading rubric for online discussions. *Journal of Online Learning and Teaching, 7* (4), 452–464.

Soliday, M. (1994). Translating self and difference through literacy narratives. *College English, 56*(5), 511.

Sommers, N. (1982). Responding to student writing. *College Composition and Communication, 33*(2), 148–156.

Sommers, N., & Saltz, L. (2004). The novice as expert: Writing the freshman year. *College Composition and Communication, 56*(1), 124–149. doi:10.2307/4140684

Stevens, D. D., & Cooper, J. E. (2009). *Journal keeping: How to use reflective writing for learning, teaching, professional insight, and positive change.* Sterling, VA: Stylus.

Stevens, D., Serap, E., & Yamashita, M. (2010). Mentoring through reflective journal writing: A qualitative study by a mentor/professor and two international graduate students. *Reflective Practice, 11*(3), 347–367.

Straub, R. (1997). Students' reactions to teacher comments: An exploratory study. *Research in the Teaching of English, 31*(1), 91–118.

Svinicki, M., & McKeachie, W. J. (2011). Meeting a class for the first time. Chapter 3 in *McKeachie's teaching tips: Strategies, research and theory for college and university teachers* (13th ed.; pp. 19–25). Belmont, CA: Wadsworth.

Swales, J. (1990). *Genre analysis: English in academic and research settings.* Cambridge, UK: Cambridge University Press.

Tobin, L. (2010). Self-disclosure as a strategic teaching tool: What I do—and don't—tell my students. *College English, 73*(2), 196–206.

Tokolahi, E. (2010). Case study: Development of a drawing-based journal to facilitate reflective Inquiry. *Reflective Practice, 11*(2), 157–170.

Tsang, A. K. L., & Walsh, L. J. (2010). Oral health students' perceptions of clinical reflective learning—Relevance to their development as evolving professionals. *European Journal of Education, 14*(2), 99–105.

Turley, E. D., & Gallagher, C. W. (2008). On the uses of rubrics: Reframing the great rubric debate. *English Journal, 97*(4), 87–92.

Ussher, B., & Earl, K. (2010). "Summative" and "formative": Confused by the assessment terms? *New Zealand Journal of Teachers' Work, 7*(1), 53–63.

van der Kolk, B. A., & van der Hart, O. (1995). The intrusive past: The flexibility of memory and the engraving of trauma. In Cathy Caruth (Ed.), *Trauma: Explorations in memory* (pp. 158–182). Baltimore, MD: Johns Hopkins University Press.

Wang, P. A. (2015). Assessment of asynchronous online discussions for a constructive online learning community. *International Journal of Information and Education Technology, 5* (8), 598–604.

Webster, D. K. (2002). *Parachute infantry: An American paratrooper's memoir of D-Day and the fall of the Third Reich*. New York, NY: Delta.

Wilhoit, S. W. (2003). *The Allyn and Bacon teaching assistant's handbook: A guide for graduate instructors of writing and literature*. New York, NY: Longman.

Wilson, J. H., & Wilson, S. B. (2007). The first day of class affects student motivation: An experimental study. *Teaching Psychology, 34*(4), 226–230.

Wyss, V. L., Freedman, D., & Siebert, C. J. (2014). The development of a discussion rubric for online courses: Standardizing expectations of graduate students in online scholarly discussions. *TechTrends, 58* (2), 99–107. http://dx.doi.org.ezproxy.pgcc.edu/10.1007/s11528-014-0741-x

Yancey, K. B. (1998). *Reflection in the writing classroom*. Logan, UT: Utah State University Press.

Index

Adams, Abigail, xii
Adams, John, xii
Alexander, Kara Poe, xiii, 37
Arter, J., 81, 82
assessment, 33, 41, 75n1, 81, 99, 102; formative commentary, 84; of narratives, 80; portfolio assessment, 59, 60; summative commentary, 84, 86n1. *See also* rubrics

Barker, Lisa M., 100, 101, 102
Bar-On, Tamir, xiii, 40
Bean, John C., 36, 88
Belanoff, Pat, 60
biography, 67, 69, 73, 74
Bullock, Richard, xiv

Carr, Nicholas, 92, 94, 95
Clark, Irene, xvii, 90
Coker, Frances H., 36
collaborative assignments, 69
Conference on College Composition and Communication (CCCC), 59, 75n1
Conway, G., 61, 64
Corkery, Caleb, xiv, 16
counternarrative, 27, 28
cover letter. *See* writing portfolios
cultural trauma, 26, 27, 28, 29n4

Davidson, Michele R., xii
Devitt, Amy J., 89, 90

diaries. *See* reflection
Dorn, Dean, xvii, 8, 11n2, 12n4
Douglass, Frederick, xi

Elbow, Peter, 60, 61

formative commentary. *See* rubrics
Frank, Anne, xii

genre, 26, 34, 35, 36, 37, 42, 43, 57, 61, 62, 86n1, 88; analyzing, 91, 92, 95, 96, 97; narrative genres, xiii, xiv, xv, xix, 16, 62, 82, 83; theory, 89, 90, 92
Goggin, Maureen Daly, 17, 18
Goggin, Peter N., 17, 18
Goodrich, Heidi, 81
Grace, Columbus M., xi

Haswell, Richard H., 99
Hawthorne, Nathaniel, 92, 93, 94, 95
Hinchman, Kathleen, xi
Hillocks, George, xiii, xvii, 40, 41

icebreakers, xix, 3, 4, 6, 11n2, 12n3, 68, 75n1
I-Search paper. *See* research

journals. *See* reflection

King, Rosamond, 7, 8

Lawson, Jenny, xii
literacy myth. *See* literacy narrative
literacy narrative, x, xi, xiii, xv, xviii, xix, 15; assigning, 19; benefits of, xiii, xiv, 16, 17; exploring trauma, xix, 16, 17, 18, 20; limitations of, xiv; literacy myth, xiv; reflection, xiii, 21, 37
Lu, Min-Zhan, 99, 101

Macrorie, Ken, 48, 55n1
McCourt, Frank, xi
McTighe, J., 81, 82
multigenre research project, 52
Murray, Donald, 38

National Council of Teachers of English (NCTE), xiv, xv
North, Stephen, xii, 35, 42, 43

O'Brien, Tim, xii
online classroom, 67, 72, 74

personification. *See* reflection

reflection, xvii, xix, 38, 48, 87, 95, 99; analysis-based, 41; assessing, 42; challenges of, 33, 37, 43; concrete objects, 40; definition of, 32, 34, 39, 43; diaries, xii; discipline-specific, 35, 36, 37, 38; journals, xii, 31, 32, 33, 34, 35, 36, 38, 41, 42; narrative-based, 33, 36, 37, 38, 39; personification, 38, 39; portfolio reflections, 61, 62, 63; types of, 33. *See also* literacy narrative
reflective introduction. *See* writing portfolios
research, xviii, xix; developing topics, 25, 32; on instructors, 8, 9, 10, 11; I-Search, 48; research-based assignments, 19, 24, 25, 26, 52, 54, 69, 70, 87; personal narratives as a catalyst for, 49, 50, 52, 54, 55; primary, 11, 32, 48, 54; questions, 11, 52; secondary, 11, 32, 48, 54
rubrics, 25, 27, 81, 99, 100, 101; analytical, 82, 83; for discussions, 101, 102, 103, 105, 106; holistic, 81, 82; for narratives, 80, 86

Saltz, Laura, 49
Sassoon, Siegfried, xii
scaffolding, 20, 54
Scarboro, Allen, 36
scenario-based discussions, 101, 102, 103, 105, 106
self-disclosure, 3, 5, 6, 7, 72, 74
Smith, Karen, xi
Soliday, Mary, xiii, xiv, 16
Sommers, Nancy, xvi, 49
storyboards, 91, 92, 93, 94, 95, 96, 97
summative commentary. *See* rubrics

teacher's assistant (TA) training, ix, x, xviii, xx, 99, 100, 102

Vedder, Eddie, xvii

Webster, David Kenyon, xii
Wilhoit, Stephen, 100
writing-intensive (WI) courses, xvii, xviii, 31, 42
writing portfolios, xix, 32, 33, 39, 57, 58, 59, 60, 61, 62, 63, 85; as narrative, 58, 60, 62, 63; cover letter, xix, 57, 58, 61, 65n2; placement portfolios, 59, 60, 61; reflective introduction, xix, 57, 58, 61, 62, 63, 64, 65n2

Yancey, Kathleen Blake, 34, 37, 39

About the Authors

Anthony Tate Fulton earned his PhD in English from Southern Illinois University–Carbondale in 2015. He has an MA in English (writing studies) from the University of Dayton and a BA in English (creative writing) from Otterbein University. He currently serves as an associate professor of English at Prince George's Community College in Largo, Maryland, where he teaches composition, technical writing, and argumentation courses.

His teaching, research, and administrative work focuses on Writing Across the Curriculum (WAC) and interdisciplinary approaches to teaching writing. At his current institution, he helps to design special topics courses, including a course on comic books and graphic novels, for the general studies program in liberal arts, in which students synthesize various disciplinary perspectives. He has also paired his argumentation course with a colleague's political science course, allowing students to apply rhetorical concepts and strategies to their political science content. In addition to his regular teaching load, he works as an assessment coach in the liberal arts division, helping faculty fulfill requirements for the institution's college-wide assessment process. In many ways, he approaches this work as a WAC consultant, promoting writing in the disciplines, shepherding more writing-based assessments, revising course outcomes, and assisting in rubric construction.

Anthony is an active member of National Council of Teachers of English (NCTE), participating in the annual conference, as well as the Conference on College Composition and Communication (CCCC). He has also presented at Drexel University's Conference on Assessment and the Composition Conversations Writing Conference. He can be reached at fultonat@pgcc.edu.

Christopher B. Field received his PhD in English from Southern Illinois University–Carbondale in 2015, his MA in English from the University of

Dayton in 2005, his BA in English from the University of Cincinnati in 2003, and his AA from Sinclair Community College in 2001. He has served as an assistant professor of English in the Languages, Literature, and Philosophy Department at Tennessee State University since 2015.

His primary area of interest is in twentieth-century American literature. He also has an active research agenda in popular culture studies—with a special interest in comics and graphic novels—as well as rhetoric and composition and early American literature.

In addition to teaching courses in American literature, comics studies, world literature, and composition, Chris also regularly attends and presents at professional conferences including the Comic Arts Conference at San Diego Comic-Con, and the Popular Culture Association / American Culture Association of the South Conference. He can be reached via email at christopher.field67@gmail.com or on Twitter @DoctorofBooks.

Michael MacBride received his PhD in English from Southern Illinois University–Carbondale in 2014, his MA in literature from Minnesota State University–Mankato, and his BS in creative writing from Eastern Michigan University. Since 2005, he has taught a variety of English, literature, and humanities courses at six different institutions.

Although his primary area of research is nineteenth-century American literature, he has additional expertise in contemporary American literature, Latin American literature, rhetoric and composition, and comic studies. This balance of course work and scholarship allows him to help students make connections across centuries, cultures, and genres and become better critical readers and thinkers about the world around them. Whether in a face-to-face, online, or hybrid setting, Michael believes it is essential that students find a personal connection to their writing.

In addition to his teaching, Michael also regularly presents at professional conferences. Two of his favorites are the NCTE Conference and the Comics Arts Conference at the San Diego Comic-Con. He can be reached via email at michael.macbride@gmail.com or on Twitter @michaelmacbride.

www.ingramcontent.com/pod-product-compliance
Lightning Source LLC
Chambersburg PA
CBHW030116010526
44116CB00005B/269